We Build Together

Third Edition

A Reader's Guide to Negro Life and Literature for Elementary and High School Use

Charlemae Rollins, Chairman of the Committee for 1967 Revision of *We Build Together*

Contributors

Augusta Baker, New York Public Library

Mildred L. Batchelder, Evanston, Illinois

Marion Edman, Wayne State University

Bertha Jenkinson, Follett Publishing Company

Effie Lee Morris, San Francisco Public Library

Eloise Rue, University of Wisconsin—Milwaukee

Marjorie B. Smiley, Hunter College of the City University of New York

Zena Bailey Sutherland, University of Chicago

Muriel Crosby, Wilmington Public Schools, Delaware, *ex officio*

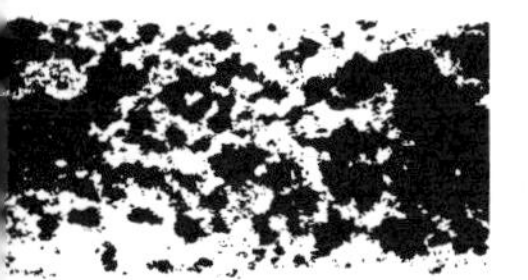

NCTE COMMITTEE ON PUBLICATIONS

CONSULTANT READERS

Elizabeth K. Burgess, Supervisor for Language Arts, Metropolitan Public Schools, Nashville–Davidson County, Tennessee

Muriel Crosby, Wilmington Public Schools, Delaware

Marie B. Dickinson, Supervisor, Los Angeles County Schools

Clementine Hamilton, Librarian, Metropolitan Public Schools, Nashville-Davidson County, Tennessee

Editing by

Cynthia H. Smith, NCTE Headquarters

Design and Art Work by

Norma Phillips, NCTE Headquarters

NATIONAL COUNCIL OF TEACHERS OF ENGLISH
508 South Sixth Street, Champaign, Illinois 61820

Foreword

We Build Together (third revision) is not just a new edition of a much needed booklist. It is a delightful short history of the changing role of the Negro in the field of literature and in American society. Between 1941, when the first edition was published, and the present date, a great social revolution has stimulated the first mass effort to assure the ultimate entrance of the Negro into the mainstream of American life.

Charlemae Rollins, chairman of the revision committee, was prime initiator of the first edition of *We Build Together* and has played a major role in each revision. In an important sense, the vast changes that have occurred in the role of the Negro in literature for children and youth is the direct result of the commitment of many teachers, librarians, and writers, among whose leaders Charlemae Rollins is without peer. Not only has she fought for a true and dignified portrayal of the Negro, but she has also devoted her talents to the writing of Negro biographies that are authentic, highly readable, and inspiring. Her delightful anthology, *Christmas Gif'*,[1] containing works about and by Negroes, portrays the Negro with dignity and humor.

Like other people, Negro writers use a vast range of styles and dialects, substandard and standard. Like other people, Negroes speak in many dialects. This Mrs. Rollins believes, knows, and reflects in *Christmas Gif'*.

The committee for the third edition of *We Build Together* has provided a splendid reference book in the important areas of human relationships and literature. Books recommended bear the test of criteria common to all good books dealing with human problems: authenticity, choices of action in solving problems, reality.

The National Council of Teachers of English is grateful to Charlemae Rollins for her leadership and for her dedication. It is proud of her and her committee for bringing a new dimension to an important tool in the education of all children. *We Build Together* should be a best seller.

MURIEL CROSBY

---

[1] Chicago: Follett Publishing Company, 1963.

Committee for 1967 Revision of We Build Together

Charlemae Rollins, former Director, Children's Department, George C. Hall Branch, Chicago Public Library, *Chairman*

Augusta Baker, Supervisor, Children's Services, New York Public Library

Mildred L. Batchelder, former Executive Secretary of Children's Services Division and Young Adult Services Division, American Library Association

G. Robert Carlsen, Professor of English and Education, University of Iowa

Marion Edman, Professor of Education, Wayne State University

Bertha Jenkinson, Editor, Children's Book Department, Follett Publishing Company

Dorothy Lawson, Young Adult Consultant, Indianapolis Public Library

Effie Lee Morris, Coordinator, Children's Library Activities, San Francisco Public Library

Eloise Rue, Professor of Education, University of Wisconsin-Milwaukee

Marjorie B. Smiley, Department of Education, Hunter College of the City University of New York

Zena Bailey Sutherland, Editor, *Bulletin*, Center for Children's Books, University of Chicago

Muriel Crosby, Acting Superintendent, Wilmington Public Schools, Delaware, *ex officio*

Acknowledgments

The Chairman of this Committee is deeply indebted to many individuals and groups for help in preparing this material for publication.

The members of the Committee read and evaluated the books (many of which do not appear on the list); some were read solely for comparison and background in judging the accepted or rejected title. Most of the members were already overloaded with important commitments of their own but nevertheless gave their time and energy in this endeavor. For these Committee members, I have no words that can adequately thank them for their many hours of hard work in reading and writing and rewriting reviews of the books sent by publishers and authors.

Special thanks go to some nonmembers who gave invaluable aid: Margaret Thomsen Raymond, author of several teenage novels and former editor of children's books for the Volland Press, who also gave editorial assistance on the first and second editions of this work and read and edited parts of the introduction for this edition; Mrs. Georgia Cowan Poole, Professor of Education, Tuskegee Institute, Alabama, and her teenage daughter Carol, who read many of the novels and sent excellent reports. Mrs. Poole also wrote a special report and evaluation of the new *Uncle Tom's Cabin.* (It has been read by Committee members also.)

Sincere thanks and appreciation go to many librarians in Chicago who made books available along with valued comments and reactions of children to controversial titles, among them Miss Marie Will, Supervisor of Work with Children, The Chicago Public Library; Mrs. Ellyn A. Hill, Librarian, Hiram Kelly Branch, The Chicago Public Library; Mrs. Dorothy Evans, Children's Librarian, Mrs. Alice Scott, Librarian, and Miss Irene Watkins, Assistant Librarian, all at the George C. Hall Branch, The Chicago Public Library.

In addition to the members of the Committee and the nonmembers, the Chairman wishes to thank Mrs. Josephine

Glover Sanders who typed and retyped copies of the many versions of the first and second editions of this publication, as well as this edition.

No less generous have been the publishers of children's books who provided copies of both old and new titles for review, helping to make this Committee's job immeasurably smoother and the annotations much more valuable.

Table of Contents

Introduction

In the process of compiling material for this third edition of *We Build Together*, the members of the Committee have been greatly heartened by the increasing number of acceptable new books from many different publishers. We were also encouraged by the numerous letters of inquiry about books on this subject.

Librarians, teachers, parents, and other adults interested in helping to strengthen the bonds of friendship between Negro youth and others have been generous in sharing with this Committee their experiences, their knowledge and opinions of books.

In this edition one does not find the labels "Recommended" and "Not Recommended." The current books published about Negroes in America are, for the most part, acceptable. The annotations help to point up the weaknesses and strengths in the books included in this bibliography and will be descriptive enough to give readers an opportunity to judge each book on an individual basis. Many have qualities that can be useful to the teacher, librarian, parent, and other adult user as well as the child.

When young children ask baffling questions such as "Why am I black?" "Why is he white?" "Why are they poor?" "Why do we move?" parents and teachers must find answers that are honest and satisfying. Artists assist through their pictures, musicians through their songs, and authors through honest portrayal of people in books.

The original edition of *We Build Together* appeared in 1941. It was intended to fill the need, often expressed by teachers, librarians, and parents, for a list of really good books for children and young people that would present Negroes as human beings and not as stereotypes. The work of the Committee preparing the first edition was arduous indeed, for few stories could be found that offered a true picture of Negroes in contemporary life—books that Negro children could enjoy without self-consciousness, books with which they could identify satisfactorily, books that white children could read and so learn what Negro young people and families were like.

After much searching, the Committee compiled a list and published a booklet of some forty-five pages containing approximately 200 titles arranged according to topic. This was eagerly received by teachers and librarians, for at that time our country was at war, fighting for the principle of full equality among all men—the central theme of the list.

One of the most valuable features of this initial list was a discussion of the criteria used by the Committee for judging the acceptability of books about Negroes. Such subjects as appropriate language, illustrations, theme, and treatment of characters were clearly delineated with examples of what was acceptable and not acceptable from various books generally popular with teachers and librarians.

The end of World War II ushered the world, including the United States, into a new era. It was now clearly recognized that the colored peoples of the world had emerged demanding equal partnership with the white minority of humankind and that they were prepared to back up their demands with appropriate action. In the United States there was a growing consciousness that the Negro must be fully integrated into American life and that the surest way to such integration was to understand him and to accept him as a fellow human being with all the privileges and responsibilities that such acceptance entails.

One of the most useful methods of helping children to understand this change in American society was to make available to them suitable books dealing with the Negro in this new light. Such emphasis encouraged writers of books for children and young people to produce more acceptable reading materials. Consequently, when *We Build Together* was revised in 1948, the Committee found a wider selection of titles available. The second list was expanded to seventy-one pages and included approximately 500 titles.

Even though the Committee had taken pains in the first edition to set guidelines for the writing and selection of acceptable books dealing with Negroes, the Committee in preparing the second edition still found many examples of poorly written and unacceptable titles. They therefore believed it wise to repeat the guidelines set up for the first edition, to make it clear again to those writing and publishing books about Negroes, and to those selecting them, that care must be taken so that the desired goals would be met. Placing such books in the hands of children carries with it responsibilities that must be recognized by writers as well as teachers, librarians, and others charged with their education. Nevertheless, the Committee was encouraged by the changes that had come about in the interval between the first and second editions—less than a decade in time—and hoped even greater changes might be brought about by stressing the original guidelines.

Now, as the Committee of the third edition attacks the problem, its members are heartened by the many developments in textbooks, history, biography, and human relations as well as in fiction, drama, and poetry, but again the Committee feels it should discuss goals for the list it hopes to present.

Heretofore many books depicting Negro life were written in an author-created dialect, difficult to read and understand. They were often illustrated with pictures that offended Negro adults and embarrassed Negro children. The stories were presented through caricatures or stereotypes. The relationships in the books between Negro and non-Negro characters were often patronizing, stressing class differences, as in stories with servant–master themes. Most Negro characters in such books were stableboys, maids, porters, or other menials. No Negro teachers, doctors, librarians, or policemen appeared in them. In many instances, the adult or juvenile Negro characters spoke in a southern dialect, whether they lived in the North, East, or West. Now, however, many books depict Negroes in all roles in our society, including the most honored ones; they live and work among all groups as equals; they are human beings with all the greatness and strengths and with all the foibles and weaknesses of mankind.

Through the books available, it is clear that the Negro's

struggle for human dignity is reflected in every facet of human life, and the fight for a place of dignity in children's literature is gradually being won by the efforts of many historians, biographers, novelists, illustrators, poets, and educators, as well as nonprofessionals who demand better books for children. The field of children's literature about Negroes now includes a growing portion of the whole field of excellent contemporary books for young people.

It has become evident that reading good books can increase the social sensitivity of a child and help him to extend his experiences to gain new insights, appreciations, and understanding of himself and others. Progress has been made in all areas of the original lists; however, more stories for younger children are needed because it is at this age that a child is introduced to the printed word and the illustrated book. These should build a firm foundation of acceptance so that the child can come to recognize that people are people in spite of their physical differences.

Stereotypes

Webster's dictionary defines a stereotype as "something conforming to a fixed or general pattern: especially a standardized mental picture held in common by members of a group and representing oversimplified opinions, affective attitude, or uncritical judgment (as of a person, a race, an issue, or an event)."

When applied to groups of people, stereotypes may be complimentary or derogatory, such as in the case of "mothers," "heroes," "the rich," "aristocracy," "Poles," or "Negroes." The danger of stereotypes is that they are untrue to reality. They dangerously simplify thinking; often they are false in their origin and certainly could not in the past or in the present be fairly applied to individual members of the group which carries the stereotype.

When stereotypes are chiefly derogatory, as has long been the case with Negroes, the oversimplified thinking which they represent is used as a valid basis for discrimination and even injustice before the law. It is, therefore, of paramount importance that books for children and young people should not reinforce the stereotypes about Negroes that are still in force, to some degree at least, in American culture. In fact, books ought to help dispel such thinking, particularly in areas where everyday contacts with members of this race are infrequent or entirely lacking. Books may serve as the only means some children and young people have of knowing what individual members of the group are *really* like.

Fortunately, many books available today do this. They picture Negroes as holding all sorts of positions, not the traditional menial ones. They are not universally of the lower class, uneducated, simple souls, often picturesque and child-like. More often now they are people faced with the universal problems of all mankind: earning a living, hating and loving, rejoicing and grieving, experiencing successes and failures, learning to find their way through a complex world of ideas, and living with other people.

The chief effect of breaking down stereotypes is to reverse the dehumanization of labeled groups. The fact that they have been looked upon as a group and not as individuals often results, especially in racial stereotyping, in attitudes that cause pain and injustice.

Television, radio, and other news media must also be commended for the conscious effort now being made to show Negroes routinely in every walk of life as Americans, fully participating at all levels. The numerous documentaries on television and radio have stimulated great interest at all levels of our society. Libraries have felt this impact through the many requests that come in from nonpatrons as well as regular library users.

Use of Language

In books dealing with Negroes, two types of language have caused concern. One is dialect; the other is false idiom. It is objectionable to portray the Negro as *always* speaking in dialect and nothing else, no matter what his station in life or his geographical location; or to write a false, author-made dialect, such as "He do," "Dis am," "Who dat?" without any basis in observation of real people and their speech.

Writers are now making a conscious effort to reproduce the natural speech of all children who are presented from any particular section of the country. The colorful speech of all who share the same economic, regional, or historical background should be reproduced as faithfully as possible in order to give flavor to the story, but never at the expense of any individual in the group.

In recent years the scientific study of language, linguistics, has thrown much light on the topic of dialect, which should be an aid to writers attempting to use this form of speech.

A branch of linguistics, dialectology, has been developed during recent years and is dedicated to the scientific study of dialects and variations among them. If the dialectologist's scientific view is understood and applied to the treatment of dialects in books for children, some changes from traditional attitudes may become necessary.

Everyone speaks a dialect of his language. Dialects may differ in the speech sounds they use, in some aspects of grammar, in vocabulary, and in idiom. Since dialects are rooted in subcultures within a general culture, they may incorporate different values, attitudes, and life views. Special ways develop for expressing the cultural view which in a real sense are not translatable into other dialects. How does "fixing to" translate to a more general term without losing something of its flavor or meaning?

Fortunately, dialects of American English differ in relatively minor ways. Most Americans understand most American dialects with little difficulty. The linguist has concluded that all dialects are equally useful in their places for the language purposes of the users. Every dialect has all the necessary attributes of a language, including a systematic grammar. It is only when judged by the norm of its own grammar that any usage may be considered incorrect within a dialect. Problems arise because certain dialects have high social values and certain others low values. Aspects of the latter are commonly held to mark the user as vulgar, ignorant, uneducated, or uncultured.

Viewed in the proper light, every dialect has form and beauty and is a potential medium of literary expression. Folklore, songs, stories, and poetry are evidence of this. Perhaps the problem with variant dialects, as they have appeared in books, has been that most often what is presented is not an accurate use of the dialect but an artificial and stereotyped version carelessly researched and used by an author unfamiliar with it. Specifically, there is no Negro dialect as such in America. There are a number of regional and social dialects spoken by Negroes and often by whites in the same areas and occupational groups. Just as a stereotyped portrayal of the Negro must be replaced by a sensitive, accurate portrayal, so the caricature of his language should be replaced by accurate, understandable use of the vernacular.

The second misuse of language has been with words that have connotations of disrespect and even contempt for all Negroes. Because of their emotional overtones, many expressions are completely repugnant to Negroes and, of course, to most well-informed whites. While these words may vary in their connotations in various parts of the country, there is a consensus that a considerable number of such words are not suitable for use in a book for young people.

Research has thrown some light on reactions to various words. Long-standing language and word habits may lead to rigid and consistent emotional responses, which appear to hold almost regardless of context. A study of racially offensive words[1] found that at least some of the 233 Negroes surveyed viewed the following words as derogatory in almost any "Negro–non-Negro" situation. The words asterisked indicate that the non-Negro sample (251 persons) viewed the words as significantly less derogatory than did the Negro.[2]

[1] R. S. Ross and G. Maddox, "Racially Potent Words: A Study to Help Locate Language Barriers to Intergroup Communication," *Speech Communication: Fundamentals and Practice* (New York: Prentice-Hall, Inc., 1965), pp. 39–40.

[2] The 0.02 level of significance.

RACIALLY POTENT WORDS

WORD	% Offensiveness (Negro)	% Offensiveness (Non-Negro)
nigger	95	92
darkie*	87	75
Sambo*	85	74
spook*	83	70
mammy*	78	52
inkspot*	73	38
Aunt Jemima*	72	43
nappy*	69	53
shine*	65	43
nigra*	65	43
you-people*	65	43
pickaninny*	65	39
black*	59	40
Sammie*	58	33
gal*	53	15
boy*	42	8
Charley*	39	8
colored	27	31
Negro	15	15

Raymond S. Ross, SPEECH COMMUNICATION: Fundamentals and Practice, © 1965. Reprinted by permission of Prentice-Hall, Inc., Englewood Cliffs, New Jersey.

The emotional interpretations attached to language demand careful audience analysis and word selection on the part of the speaker. Words are not things or emotions, but we often act as if they were. Language is by nature abstract and involves generalizations about concrete or real things: the writer's job is to deemphasize words which, particularly in certain contexts, may strain relations between individuals and groups.

Illustrations

Of major importance in evaluating books about Negroes for young people are the illustrations. In the two earlier versions of this list—1941 and 1948—much was made of the unfortunate stereotyped illustrations appearing in even the books with texts sympathetic to minorities. Artists usually depicted Negroes with thick lips, bulbous noses, and hair done up in turbans, eternally eating watermelon. A Negro mother might carry baskets of laundry, but never bags of groceries; a father might sweep streets, but never carry a briefcase!

It was this cultural stereotyping that sensitive critics objected to; Negroes might be unskilled laborers, pickers of cotton, or guitar-playing buffoons, but never scholars or doctors, or even shopkeepers, policemen, firemen, or postmen. Yet Negroes had long filled such posts with honor and dignity and distinction.

Pictures of Negro children and grownups in books have, over the years, improved mightily. This is especially true of books written and illustrated by Elizabeth Orton Jones, Marguerite De Angeli, Ezra Jack Keats, and others. Among the first good books with excellent illustrations and texts suitable for small children to be read by themselves were the Eva Knox Evans stories of *Araminta*, with their lively black-and-white drawings. A similarly illustrated book of a more recent date is *Mississippi Possum* by Miska Miles, illustrated by John Schoenherr. Frequently, in current books for all ages, no mention is made of cultural or racial background; only by the illustrations is the reader made aware of differences. *Two Is a Team* (1945), by Lorraine and Jerrold Beim, illustrated by Ernest Crichlow, first used this device. Nowhere in the text is any mention made of the fact that one boy is white and the other is a Negro. Yet both are in the same trouble for having caused a series of disasters with their wagon; and both make repayment "as a team." It is this simple device, so much appreciated when it first appeared by all who were aware of the importance of such an advance, that has had a profound effect on children's illustrations and continues to do so.

Because *Little Black Sambo*, written and illustrated by Helen Bannerman (1901), has both pictures and text which have given great delight to white children the world over, it was included in the earliest (1941) list. For a time, it was the only picture book in which a dark-skinned child was the hero. Only mild objections were raised by sensitive readers to the story or the pictures. As the years passed, more and more adults, both Negro and white, recognized how much Negro children were stereotyped by the word "black" and the epithet "Sambo." This name, characterizing a clownish Negro, was used in minstrel shows long before Mrs. Bannerman's time and was undoubtedly familiar to her in this context, no matter how innocently she may have used it. A white author using stereotyped names such as George for a waiter or a pullman car porter, or Dinah for a woman who works by the day, ought to reexamine his attitudes to learn in what areas his prejudices still linger.

Little Black Sambo, because of the many objections raised to its inclusion on the early list, became for the compilers of *We Build Together* a symbol and a yardstick by which to measure contemporary books.

It was the strong stand taken generally by librarians, teachers, and parents against stereotypes that is responsible for the change which has come in the many fine illustrated books now available.

Though the picture book list is short in this bibliography, it must be noted that two Caldecott winners appear there. *The Snowy Day*, by Ezra Jack Keats, has a Negro child as its hero. *A Prayer for a Child*, by Rachel Field and illustrated by Elizabeth Orton Jones, includes Negro children among the world's children. It is also important to note that the objectionable double-page spread with the illustration showing a clearly stereotyped Negro child—barefooted, ragged, and with hound in attendance—has been deleted from the recent reprinting of *The Rooster Crows* by the Petershams, also a Caldecott winner.

In this trend toward the non-stereotyped illustration, we have not only excellent realistic pictures and photographs, but also imaginative and delightful illustrations in the modern manner, such as the Ezra Jack Keats books. This trend, for which we all cannot be too grateful, is now extended so that Negro children are incidentally included in all types of readers, picture books, science texts, beginning-to-read stories, historical material—just as they truly are represented in this way in most of our major cities, schools, and even in many rural areas today.

Folklore

American folklore is rich in stories, poems, songs, games, work-songs, play-songs and game-songs of all groups of people who make up our country, although Indian myths are considered to be the only really authentic American folklore.

The contributions made by the American Negro have African roots. Negroes were able to bring with them when they came to America only their memories of life in Africa, memories kept alive by their songs and stories told in broken English to each other. Many of these stories have never been written for children. A small part of this rich heritage was luckily saved by Joel Chandler Harris in his *Tales of Uncle Remus*, but a great deal must have been lost in the retelling and in Harris' own interpretation of the stories attributed to an old slave whom Harris named "Uncle Remus," for he used his character as a means of furthering his own ideas of chiding the slave for wanting to escape and for stealing food when he was hungry. These features of the "Tales" have made the stories objectionable to many Negroes.

In her book, *Joel Chandler Harris, Folklorist* (University of Georgia Press, 1950), Dr. Stella Brewer Brooks has analyzed those of the Uncle Remus tales which can be called folktales. These tales have been directly traced to their African counterparts. Some of the themes used here are found in the folklore of other peoples.

The originals of some of the Uncle Remus stories have been criticized and judged objectionable by Negroes and other educators for reasons other than Harris' personal biases. Although they were written in an authentic Negro dialect true to the period in which they appeared, the dialect also includes the objectionable and derogatory terms "nigger," "darkie," "coon," and "pickaninny." Harris has also been criticized because he used Uncle Remus to portray the slave as leading a happy, contented life. In some of the tales the slaves are pictured as dishonest; they steal food and lie about each other to curry favor with their masters.

Margaret Wise Brown, in her adaptation of some of the

stories for children in *Bre'r Rabbit* (Harper, 1941), has helped to make Uncle Remus more acceptable for use with today's youth. She has simplified the dialect and omitted most of the objectionable language.

Epaminondas is an American version of a very familiar European folk character who is lovable, literal-minded, and childlike. The story is humorous and full of action, and the outlandish name is loved by children. It has the repetitious nonsense that they enjoy, and the humor is childlike and wholesome. However, such words as "auntie" and "mammy" give it a condescending tone. The illustrations have usually been even more objectionable than the language in the various editions generally available to children.

Nicodemus is a character often mistaken for a folklore figure, but he is a creation of the author, Inez Hogan. This series of stories is about a little boy and poor, ragged, unkempt, and ignorant children on a plantation, with objectionable illustrations and ungrammatical language. Unlike the Uncle Remus dialect, it has the contemporary southern speech of both whites and Negroes.

Little Black Sambo is an imaginative story, not a folk tale, since there are no traditional sources. It does have wonderful dramatic qualities such as rhythm, repetition, and rollicking humor. The little boy is a hero; he outwits the tigers; he eats an enormous number of pancakes; he leaves some hearts hurt if not broken, but he is also a harmful, objectionable stereotype. "Black" coupled with "Sambo" doubles the objection and creates a stereotype of a slow, stupid, barefoot, ugly person, who becomes a "character" and not a figure in a folk tale.

John Henry is a folk hero, a Negro who deserves a place beside Paul Bunyan, Pecos Bill, Mike Fink, and Davy Crockett. He is best portrayed by the vigorous humor of James Daugherty in his version *John Henry and the Double-Jointed Steam Drill,* and in *John Henry and His Hammer* by Harold Felton. Both of these books are excellent for storytelling or reading aloud. A recent version for both young and old is *John Henry: An American Legend* by the Caldecott Award winner Ezra Jack Keats.

Additional acceptable Negro folk characters are Stack-O-Lee and Molly Means, a Negro woman. These characters are described in a prize-winning poem by Margaret Walker, a Negro poet. The verses are more suitable for older boys and girls since the characters are described rather realistically in her rhythmic *For My People* (Yale University Press, 1942).

Biography and History

Reading the life stories of famous people can help children to identify with and share the experiences of the person written about. Insights can be gained from sharing in the disappointment of Marian Anderson who was not allowed to sing in Constitution Hall on Easter, or of George Washington Carver who was not permitted to eat in the Senate restaurant in Washington. Likewise, readers can rejoice in the triumphs of these same persons in other circumstances.

The understanding which accrues from a stored experience, even one that happened in early childhood, can be applied to the immediate situations that young people face. The field of biography is by far the most helpful in this regard compared to any manner of presentation. It is also the most acceptable and includes the greatest number of Negro authors. It is here that all children can build a firm foundation of knowledge of and respect for Negroes. They will be prepared for the first introduction to the concept of different skin color. The Negro child will be better prepared to face the realities of life: that in some circumstances he will be successful, in other situations not. His successes and failures may or may not have something to do with his race. The lives of the Negro heroes, both past and contemporary, have opened the eyes of Negroes and given them an urgent sense of pride in the accomplishments of their forebears. They now can feel that America is indeed their country.

Librarians working with children and young people find themselves taxed to keep abreast of the continuing requests for materials on the lives of Negroes, both historical and contemporary. "I saw this on TV," or "I heard this documentary and I want material on the Negro," is now heard constantly in libraries across the country. Collections of clippings from magazines and newspapers which are kept up-to-date must sometimes substitute for scarce book material.

The story of the Negro in America includes some of the most dramatic and colorful episodes in our history. It begins with the group of Africans who were kidnapped and shipped aboard the *Long Black Schooner* (by Emma Gelders Sterne); the voyage is documented by Arna Bontemps in his *Story of the Negro. Captain of the Planter*, by Dorothy Sterling, is a thrilling account of one of the most daring episodes in American history. *Railroad to Freedom* (the life of Harriet Tubman), by Hildegarde Swift, includes in this new edition a useful bibliography with a special note on the use of the words "nigger," "darkie," "kinky," etc. Historical stories such as *Railroad to Freedom* were the forerunners of the many good historical novels and biographies we have included in our bibliography.

Today's young people should know that the fight for integration of Negroes in American schools is not new. It first began in 1831 when Prudence Crandall, a young Quaker teacher, admitted a free Negro girl to her "exclusive school" for young white girls in Canterbury, Connecticut. Elizabeth Yates's *Prudence Crandall: Woman of Courage* is a tender love story which teenagers will enjoy, as well as appreciating its historical background. Such books should and must be included on lists of books about our country, our heritage, and our way of life.

It is very heartening to see that the *Childhood of Famous Americans* series includes the biographies of three Negroes, Booker T. Washington, George Washington Carver, and Crispus Attucks. These slight little books are popular with younger children and with slow readers among the older boys and girls.

Incidents in the lives of Phillis Wheatley, Harriet Tubman, Frederick Douglass, Sojourner Truth, Benjamin Banneker, and others are suggested to publishers and writers as opportunities to give younger children a few more Negro American heroes.

Fiction

Since 1948, certain clear trends have emerged in fiction about Negroes for children and young people at all levels. Of the more than 2000 juvenile books published annually, only a small percentage are concerned with racial minorities, particularly Negroes. Yet almost every important publishing house now has one or more books on its list either touching on the subject or concerned with the issues of integration, segregation, and impoverishment, or participation in the vision of the "Great Society."

It is natural that the books for young people of junior high school age about these problems should be more plentiful than those for younger children and that they should face the issues more squarely.

Three of the most recent and penetrating are *Durango Street* by Frank Bonham, *Jazz Country* by Nat Hentoff, and *Lions in the Way* by Bella Rodman. *Durango Street,* although it was published before the Watts riots in the summer of 1965, could well have been about that area. *Jazz Country* is a candid story about racial attitudes in musical circles; and *Lions in the Way* tells of the integration of a high school in a southern border town and the experiences of eight young Negroes.

Another teenage novel which faces up to the sober realities of contemporary life is *Masquerade* by Dorothy Butters. This is about a group of girls in a Philadelphia art school who discover the meaning of prejudice when one is found to be a Negro. *South Town* by Lorenz Graham is about a southern boy who longs to be a doctor, and whose family is forced to move north because of violence. Its sequel, *North Town,* has the newly arrived David and his family struggling with the problems of jobs, school, and gangs.

Mary Jane by Dorothy Sterling was a forerunner of this trend and is still one of the most popular stories on school integration. A more recent book on the subject, for somewhat younger children, is Natalie Carlson's *The Empty Schoolhouse.* Integration of a Catholic grade school in the South is the theme. The first-person telling by an older sister gives the story warmth and charm.

For even younger children, there is *New Boy in School* by May Justus which tells of the loneliness of a brown-skinned first grader in an all-white room.

Housing is another important issue in the lives of all of us. *The House at 12 Rose Street* by Mimi Brodsky, illustrated by the Negro artist David Hodges, centers on all the difficulties of the first Negro family in a "good" middle-class neighborhood. For his friendship with the new boy, the twelve-year-old Boy Scout hero of the story is attacked and beaten. Like many good stories, the ending leaves one feeling that all has not been resolved, but that the first giant steps forward have been taken.

A Question of Harmony by Gretchen Sprague is not only concerned with anti-racial feeling, but with anti-Semitism, which descends on three talented young people. *Who Wants Music on Monday?* by Mary Stolz is reviewed elsewhere in this book as "a moving and intelligent book, perceptive in its analysis of family relationships, candid in its appraisal of race relations, true in its characterization." *Pastures of the Blue Crane* by Hesba Fay Brinsmead has an Australian background but has been included because it is the only book we know which deals candidly with "mixed blood," and because it has the deeper message of the innate worth of the individual.

For the fifth and sixth grades, few books have reached the high standard set by *Bright April*, written and illustrated by Marguerite De Angeli. *Roosevelt Grady* by Louisa R. Shotwell is about a migratory family which dreams of a permanent home. There are fewer books for this age group about the contemporary scene, unfortunately. One of great beauty is *A Certain Small Shepherd*, a Christmas story, by Rebecca Caudill. The handsome and imaginative illustrations by William Pène Du Bois help to make it even more special. Jamie, a small boy who is a mute, learns to speak through the miracle of birth on Christmas. The first indication that the couple at the door who are seeking shelter from the storm are Negro is a snowy picture—the text makes no mention of it.

A Ride on High by Candida Palmer is about two boys riding on an elevated train who find an ingenious way to solve the loss of a return fare.

The humorous turn of events in *Who's in Charge of Lincoln?* by Dale Fife is made even more funny by the matter-of-fact way in which Lincoln proceeds to travel from New York to Washington without adult escort or money! This book is important not only for its humor but for the fact that it is about a middle-class family living in New York.

When *Two Is a Team* by the Beims was published in 1945, it was unique. Other books which ignore color, taking it for granted that it is of no importance in human relations, are just beginning to appear in significant numbers. Few books have equaled it in popularity. We now have Ezra Jack Keats's wonderful picture books for the very youngest, the Caldecott winner, *The Snowy Day*, and the tender and delightful *Whistle for Willie*. His *John Henry* is for somewhat older children.

A simple story, easy to read, is *What Mary Jo Shared* by Janice May Udry. It should help the shy child, who hesitates to participate in the sharing time in kindergarten. It is a moving and altogether charming idea that Mary Jo wants to share her father. Again the fact that Mary Jo's family is Negro is shown only through the illustrations.

Among the beginning-to-read books, there are a growing number of good stories, delightfully funny, where children are children—all colors, sizes, and shapes!

Negro children can now identify more often with fictional characters who are doing normal things, common to *all* children, and can begin to see themselves as playing and living near children of every type of religious, national, or racial origin—whether they are living in the city or country, East, West, North, or South.

Our emphasis here has been on contemporary fiction, because historical fiction has always been more in evidence. These are fully discussed in the individual annotations. The greatest strides have been made in stories which portray the current scene, and we have tried to point out the coming to grips with reality.

Poetry

The contribution of Negro poets to American poetry is well known. It had its beginning with Phillis Wheatley in the eighteenth century and is now evidenced by the volumes on the shelves of our libraries. We name only a few of the best known: Paul Laurence Dunbar, James Weldon Johnson, Countee Cullen, Langston Hughes, and Pulitzer Prize winner Gwendolyn Brooks. Biographies and collections of their works are included in the bibliography.

Nonfiction

A long overdue development can be seen in all nonfiction books for children. All types of nonfiction are beginning to show Negroes in the illustrations as participating in all facets of American life—social, economic, and geographic.

The greatest strides have been made in science books, where we now have a continuation of what was begun by the anthropologists and such writers as Eva Knox Evans in her *All about Us*. Even for the youngest children, we now have a candid discussion of skin color and hair texture.

There is still a dearth of books on Negro scientists' contributions, and we continue to get mainly biographical material on the same few.

Sports

The achievements made by Negroes in the popular sports have been spectacular. Many fiction and nonfiction books in which Negroes appear help to support the idea that one's ability matters far more than his color. In sports, as in music and entertainment, young people are influenced by this idea; and of course the typically American love of sportsmanship adds further support.

What of the Future?

Even greater evidence that children's books are not written in a vacuum but reflect the changing times is the revisions which have been made on three important books long in print.

Derogatory terms, such as "nigger," "darkie," "coon," and "pickaninny," have been deleted from *The Story of Doctor Dolittle,* by Hugh Lofting. Two pages with objectionable pictures and language were removed from *The Rooster Crows,* by the Petershams. *Uncle Tom's Cabin* has been adapted, in an attractive new edition, by Anne Terry White. Mrs. White has substituted acceptable words for objectionable ones, deleted diverting and irrelevant passages, and simplified sentence structure, making the book more readable for young people.

Many of the textbook publishers have modified their readers to include multi-ethnic pictures, and they are beginning to be aware of the need to include the role of the Negro throughout our history—a role which has often been completely ignored or misrepresented.

Legislation integrating schools and materials further strengthens the position of librarians, teachers, publishers, and civil rights workers who are conscientiously trying to portray every segment of our population honestly and sincerely. Everything points to the fact that we can look forward to more and better books on the Negro for everyone.

In this edition, it has not been necessary to include every book for children ever published on the Negro in America, as was true in the first edition. In the 1948 edition we also included books for the high school student, but today these students have such a wide range of adult material that it was impossible to include adult books as part of our bibliography. The present list includes books for the preschool child to the ninth grade in the junior high school.

Some of the old titles are now out of print and some have been superseded by better titles, so that it has been possible to be more selective. The committee is aware that grading a book is an arbitrary decision and has adopted the American Library Association's scheme of a spread of three grades where possible. Teachers and librarians will, of course, be able to judge which are most suitable for slow or accelerated readers. In the annotations we have tried to point out these classifications.

Designating a title for a particular category is also arbitrary when the book could have been assigned to more than one subject area; in some cases books appear more than once.

Titles within each category are alphabetically arranged except in the case of biographies, which are arranged by subject.

Prices were checked in the 1966 *Books in Print*, the edition current as the book went to press in fall 1967. When possible we have listed trade and library editions. We have included some of the paperback editions, but teachers would do well to check new editions of *Paperbacks in Print*, as there is a steady increase in the number of juvenile titles available in these editions.

CHARLEMAE ROLLINS and
MARION EDMAN

Picturebooks and Easy-to-Read Books

WHAT IS A CHILDREN'S BOOK? It is a plum in Jack Horner's pie. It is a stolen hour in a racing day. It is a run through a wind-brushed field. It is the mystery of a cave unventured. It is the sharpness of a crisp, clear dawn. It is the joy of sun in a secret place. It is awareness in a tall forest. It is the magic of wishes cast into a starry night. It is a dream that winds into the fog of tomorrow. It is the fearful wonder of aloneness. It is a crowd laughing in unity. It is tears wept in quiet. It is life and death and a thousand lives all given to one.

This is a children's book: the bearer of all dreams, all hopes; the completion of today and a grope toward tomorrow; every child reaching toward himself as he will be or as he would be.

—JEAN KARL, 1963

ALIKI (Aliki Brandenberg). A WEED IS A FLOWER: THE LIFE OF GEORGE WASHINGTON CARVER. Illustrated by the author. Prentice, 1965. $4.25. K–3

A read-aloud picturebook biography of the great scientist. The writing style is rather stilted but adequate; the coverage is light but gives a fairly balanced picture of Dr. Carver as a person and of his research and teaching. The illustrations are most attractive in their composition and use of color, but many of them seem curiously unrealistic, since the faces seem Polynesian or Indian rather than Negro. Some of the pictures of Dr. Carver look very little like him. One happy departure from the usual color illustrations appears: Aliki paints her characters in a realistic range of skin tones.

BEIM, JERROLD. SWIMMING HOLE. Illustrated by Louis Darling. Morrow, 1951. Library binding $2.94 net. K–3

A small picture book that humorously ridicules "color prejudice" in such a way that the youngest child can understand its point.

BEIM, LORRAINE and JERROLD. TWO IS A TEAM. Illustrated by Ernest Crichlow. Harcourt, 1945. $2.75. K–3

Simple, readable story of friendship and cooperation between two small boys. Only through the illustrations does one learn that this is an interracial theme.

A read-aloud story as well as a book for the beginning independent reader. Illustrated by the Negro artist Ernest Crichlow.

BONSALL, CROSBY NEWELL. CASE OF THE HUNGRY STRANGER. Illustrated. Harper, 1963. $1.95. (Library binding $2.19 net) (I Can Read mystery) K–2

Four young friends, one of whom is a Negro boy, help find Mrs. Meech's missing blueberry pies. Told with delightful humor and originality, this story is an example of a Negro child included in a group with only the pictures indicating his color.

A good story for the beginning independent reader.

————. CASE OF THE CAT'S MEOW. Illustrated. Harper, 1965. $1.95. (Library binding $2.19 net) (I Can Read book) K–2

A small boy's slightly older friends laugh at him when he tries to convince them that his cat, Mildred, is so special that someone may steal her. But, when Mildred disappears mysteriously, they help him search for her. When she is found, they share her kittens.

Amusing situation, childlike dialogue, and the funny illustrations will delight beginning readers. Children will also understand Snitch's devotion to his out-of-the-ordinary cat. The illustrations show all kinds of boys. Can be read to younger children.

BRENNER, BARBARA. BEEF STEW. Illustrated. Knopf, 1965. $3.25. (Library binding $2.99 net) K–3

An engaging book for the beginning reader, this story is more realistic than eventful but gives a good picture of family and community life. Since he knows they are having beef stew, Nicky asks his mother if he may bring a friend home for dinner. One friend has a dental appointment, another doesn't like beef stew, the school librarian has to cook for her husband; then—O joy!—Nicky's grandmother comes for a visit and a dinner of beef stew. The very pleasant illustrations show that the school librarian is a young Negro woman.

BROWN, JEANETTE PERKINS. RONNIE'S WISH. Illustrated by Jean Martinez. Friendship, 1954. $1.50. (Paper $.95) Preschool–3

A small Negro boy has interesting adventures in the children's zoo.

BURCHARDT, NELLIE. PROJECT CAT. Illustrated by Fermin Rocker. Watts, 1966. Library binding $2.95. 1–5

Betsy and her friends discover a gray-and-white tabby cat under the bushes on the city housing project. Animals are forbidden, but the children of several nationalities and races love her and feed her when they discover her injured paw.

As the days go by and there definitely will be kittens, hiding her from the maintenance men becomes difficult. Finally they are able to get a petition to the mayor and council and have the ban on pets repealed.

CAUDILL, REBECCA. A CERTAIN SMALL SHEPHERD. Illustrated by William Pène Du Bois. Holt, 1965. $3.50. (Library binding $3.27 net) All grades

Motherless Jamie, surrounded by a loving family, is a mute. His father is convinced that one day he will talk. When an understanding teacher makes him a shepherd in the Christmas pageant, Jamie lives for that day. A severe storm dashes his joy. A Negro couple seek shelter (they have been turned away at three houses), and Jamie's father takes them to the warm church across the road. When the baby is born, the excited Jamie puts on his shepherd's robe and brings the baby a Christmas gift, saying clearly, "Here's a gift for the Child."

This moving story, set in the mountains of Appalachia, tells only through the lovely drawings that the wandering couple are Negroes. The text only intimates this in a subtle way, giving the writing a dramatic and emotional quality which makes this a Christmas story filled with love and faith.

GIPSON, FRED. TRAIL-DRIVING ROOSTER. Illustrated by Marc Simont. Harper, 1955. $2.95. All grades

A boisterous tall tale about a scrawny rooster named Dick whose fighting spirit saves him from the frying pan. He rewards his friend, the Negro cook, by helping the white crew to teach a lesson to a cafe owner who refused to serve the cook in Dodge City.

The author has combined several versions of Dick's story with all the flavor of the authentic American tall tale. The illustrator is a Caldecott Award-winning artist. Excellent read-aloud story.

GOLDIN, AUGUSTA. STRAIGHT HAIR, CURLY HAIR. Illustrated by Ed Emberley. Crowell, 1966. $3.25. (Library binding $2.96 net) (Let's-Read-and-Find-Out book) K–3

An easy-to-read scientific explanation of why some hair is straight and some curly. The humorous drawings add interest to a subject about which most children are curious.

GRIFALCONI, ANN. CITY RHYTHMS. Illustrated by the author. Bobbs, 1965. $4.95. (Library binding $4.25 net) 1–3

A handsomely illustrated book about the exciting sounds of the city on a hot summer day. Jimmy, a little Negro boy, suddenly becomes aware of the sounds of the subway, the market place, the pigeons on the roof, and the many other rhythms of the things about him as he listens intently.

A delightful combination of text and pictures which will appeal to the small child's sense of wonder and imagination; teachers will find it useful for reading aloud.

HOGAN, INEZ. NAPPY HAS A NEW FRIEND. Illustrated by the author. Dutton, 1947. $1.75. K–3

Inez Hogan has presented this little Negro character in an appealing story of friendship and cooperation. Illustrations in this book are quite different from this author's objectionable *Nicodemus* stories.

KEATS, EZRA JACK. JOHN HENRY: AN AMERICAN LEGEND. Illustrated by the author. Pantheon, 1965. $3.50. (Library binding $3.39 net) K–3

A simplified picturebook version of the legend of the Negro folk hero. The illustrations are superb, with their broad areas of color on the double-page spreads. The paintings are filled with warmth, vitality, and humor. Lends itself to reading aloud.

———. THE SNOWY DAY. Illustrated by the author. Viking, 1962. $3.00. (Library binding $2.96 net) Preschool–3

Delightful pictorial account of a small child's first experiences in the snow. Peter plays alone in the snow, discovering all the wonderful surprises and the magic of a snowball which disappears when put in a coat pocket.

Awarded the Caldecott Medal in 1962 for "the most distinguished picture book of the year," this is the first of the Caldecott Award-winning books to show an appealing American Negro child as the leading character.

———. WHISTLE FOR WILLIE. Illustrated by the author. Viking, 1964. $3.50. (Library binding $3.37 net) Preschool–K

Small children will identify readily with Peter's desire to learn how to whistle. When he finally succeeds, they will know exactly why he whistled not only for his dog, Willie, but all the way to the grocery store and back.

The color and design seem even more impressive than those in *The Snowy Day*. A *New York Times* reviewer said that this "is very likely a profound lesson for a young white child—that a human being can be a Negro without having anyone remark on the fact."

KESSLER, LEONARD P. HERE COMES THE STRIKEOUT. Illustrated. Harper, 1965. $1.95. (Library binding $2.19 net) K–3

A delightful book for beginning independent readers, the engaging illustrations showing Willie, the friend and mentor of the strikeout king (Bobby, a white boy), to be Negro. Bobby, in despair because his batting is weak, tries Willie's lucky hat. No luck! Then Willie coaches Bobby, who practices and practices and finally gets a hit—no instant success, but a combination of hard work and encouragement from Willie. The home attitude is good, too.

LERNER, MARGUERITE RUSH. RED MAN, WHITE MAN, AFRICAN CHIEF: THE STORY OF SKIN COLOR. Illustrated. Lerner, 1960. $2.75 1–5

A good introduction to the reason for difference in skin color. The style is objective and simple, and the book is well illustrated.

LEXAU, JOAN M. BENJIE. Illustrated by Don Bolognese. Dial, 1964. $3.00. (Library binding $2.97) 2–4

A book about a small, shy Negro boy who lives with his grandmother and who is too timid to speak to other people. One day his grandmother loses a treasured earring, and Benjie goes hunting for it. Because he is thinking of Granny, not himself, he speaks; once he has begun, he finds that it is both easy and pleasant to talk to people. The quick change is not really convincing, although the motivation is sound; the picture drawn of a warm relationship between the generations is most appealing.

————. I SHOULD HAVE STAYED IN BED! Illustrated by Syd Hoff. Harper, 1965. $2.50. (Library binding $2.57 net) K–2

Sam awakens late and from then on everything goes wrong—at home and school. Told with a gay simplicity in the first person, this will appeal to beginning readers because it is a familiar situation told entertainingly. The pictures are the only indication that Sam and others in his class are Negroes.

LIPKIND, WILLIAM, and N. MORDVINOFF. FOUR-LEAF CLOVER. Illustrated by the authors. Harcourt, 1959. $3.00. K–3

Mark and Peter need a bit of luck, so they hunt for a four-leaf clover. A bull charges; they land in a tree, climb down on a horse, and are thrown over the horse's head into barrels on a truck. These roll off and down a hill. A goat butts them onto a fence, and they relax and admire the lucky clover leaf. Only the illustrations show that one boy is Negro.

MCBROWN, GERTRUDE PARTHENIA. PICTURE POETRY BOOK. Illustrated by Lois Jones. Associated, 1935. $1.40. K–3

Simple verses, attractively illustrated by a Negro artist. One of the earliest works of its kind which is still useful.

MARTIN, PATRICIA MILES. THE LITTLE BROWN HEN. Illustrated by Harper Johnson. Crowell, 1960. $2.50. (Library binding $2.40 net) Preschool–3

A small Negro boy has a favorite pet, Little Brown Hen. One morning the little hen disappears. His family and friends help him search, but finally when he goes off to fish—as he always does when he is worried—he finds his pet.

An easy-to-read story which will appeal to younger children because of its warm and understanding portrayal of a small boy. Harper Johnson's realistic black-and-white drawings capture the feeling of the story.

MILES, MISKA. MISSISSIPPI POSSUM. Illustrated by John Shoenherr. Little, 1965. $3.00. (Library binding $2.97 net) 1–5

There is much that this particular possum fears, including people, but the flood brings him to Rose Mary and her family. Rose Mary feeds him, and gradually and naturally he loses his fear. Although the story is a quiet one, children will find themselves emotionally involved through the dramatic and simple text and the unusually fine illustrations, which show the Jackson family to be Negroes. The many pictures and fairly short text make this good for reading to the primary grades.

NEWSOME, EFFIE LEE. GLADIOLA GARDEN. Illustrated by Lois Jones. Associated, 1940. $2.65. K–3

Poems for younger children by a Negro poet and artist.

NORFLEET, MARY CROCKETT. HAND-ME-DOWN HOUSE. Knox, 1962. $2.00. 1–3

Jakie is a seven-year-old Negro boy who makes friends with the elderly white lady living next door; thus he helps his family adjust to their new home in a racially changing neighborhood.

PALMER, CANDIDA. A RIDE ON HIGH. Illustrated. Lippincott, 1966. $2.95. (Library binding $2.82 net) K–3

An urban story, rather pedestrian in writing style but particularly useful in the way it shows the resourcefulness of the young. Two small Negro boys, Chet and Tony, set off on the elevated train to see a ball game. Tony loses the return trip token, and the boys worry about getting home, but together they work out a way. Attractive illustrations.

RANDALL, BLOSSOM. FUN FOR CHRIS. Illustrated by Eunice Young Smith. Whitman, 1956. $1.75. Sightsaving edition available. Preschool–3

In a way that is completely satisfying, a simple story explains to a small child the difference in skin color. Two little boys, one a Negro, are playing happily when a neighbor child refuses to join the fun. Chris's mother explains in a straightforward manner that skin color differs just as flowers and other forms of life differ.

SCOTT, ANN HERBERT. BIG COWBOY WESTERN. Illustrated by Richard W. Lewis. Lothrop, 1965. $2.95. (Library binding $2.84 net) K–2

Martin lives with his mother and four sisters in a modern highrise project. On his fifth birthday he is given a cowboy outfit. All he lacks is a horse. His make-believe world is complete when the old-fashioned fruit-and-vegetable man lets him take charge of his horse. A delightful story set in an interracial housing project, attractively landscaped and well maintained.

A read-aloud picturebook.

SELSAM, MILLICENT E. TONY'S BIRDS. Illustrated by Kurt Werth. Harper, 1961. $1.95. (Library binding $2.19 net) Paper $.88. (I Can Read book) K–3

Tony becomes interested in bird-watching while on a walk with his father. The author successfully combines story and scientifically accurate information. The illustrations show that Tony is a Negro. Excellent example of good science information for the beginning reader.

One of the earliest titles in which the child's color is evident only in the attractive illustrations.

SHACKELFORD, JANE D. MY HAPPY DAYS. Illustrated with photographs. Associated, n.d. $2.65. K–3

A large, photographic picturebook—a forerunner of its kind—which shows the daily activities of a middle-class Negro family in a city.

SHARPE, STELLA GENTRY. TOBE. Illustrated with photographs by Charles Farrell. University of North Carolina Press, 1939. $2.79. K–3

A large, photographic picturebook about Tobe, a Negro boy who lives on a farm in the South. Although the book was published more than twenty-five years ago, it is still typical of home and family life, church, and holiday celebrations in certain isolated rural Negro communities, without stereotyping,

SHOWERS, PAUL. LOOK AT YOUR EYES. Illustrated by Paul Galdone. Crowell, 1962. $3.25. (Library binding $2.96 net) (Let's-Read-and-Find-Out book) K–3

Children learn through easy text and attractive illustrations some of the basic facts about the eyes. The child pictured is a Negro, and comparison of eye color is made by picturing his friends.

————. YOUR SKIN AND MINE. Illustrated by Paul Galdone. Crowell, 1965. $3.25. (Library binding $2.96 net) (Let's-Read-and-Find-Out book) K–3

The simple, brief text and attractive illustrations present the basic facts about skin and its functions, including color differences, the dermis and epidermis, hair follicles, pores, sensation and temperature adjustments, etc. The discussion of color differences and the use of boys of different color are natural parts of the text and illustrations. Large print and attractive format.

Useful as a book to be read to small children to answer one of the most frequently asked questions: "Why is his skin a different color?"

TARRY, ELLEN, and MARIE HALL ETS. MY DOG RINTY (rev. ed.). Photographs by Alland. Viking, 1962. $3.00. (Library binding $2.96 net) K–4

Back in print after some years when it was unavailable, this book is about David's adventures with his dog, who turns out to be a profitable mouse-catcher.

Splendid photographs and a dramatic story give a good picture of Harlem.

TAYLOR, SYDNEY. THE DOG WHO CAME TO DINNER. Illustrated by John E. Johnson. Follett, 1966. $1.00. (Library binding $1.83 net) K–3

This is the story of two families, each of them under the impression that the large, obstreperous dog that is blighting a dinner party belongs to the other. The Browns and Lanes seem inordinately patient with the animal, whose misbehavior culminates in licking plates at the dinner table. Then they discover he has just walked in with the Lanes; they are new neighbors who are visiting for the first time. The Lanes are Negro, their hosts are not; the story happily assumes that it is a natural gesture of welcome to the new family next door to invite them to dinner. The illustrations show attractive young families, each with a boy and a girl.

UDRY, JANICE MAY. WHAT MARY JO SHARED. Illustrated by Eleanor Mill. Whitman, 1966. $2.95. 1–3

An easy-to-read story about Mary Jo who wants to participate in "sharing time" at school but is shy and cannot think of something that has not already been shared. Finally she thinks of sharing her physician father. Mary Jo is an appealing little girl who happens to be Negro. The writing is smooth and natural, and the illustrations, done in soft colors and black and white, are charming.

VOGEL, ILSE-MARGRET. HELLO, HENRY. Illustrated by the author. Parents, 1965. $2.95. (Library binding $3.03 net) K–2

Two young boys named Henry, whose mothers have become lost in the supermarket, play together contentedly until their mothers find them again. Theirs is a friendship upon first sight, and the fact that one boy is white and one is Negro is handled with ease, simply and realistically.

An imaginative picturebook with bright pictures. Good for reading aloud.

WILLIAMSON, STAN. NO-BARK DOG. Illustrated by Tom O'Sullivan. Follet, 1962. $1.00. 1–3

A lighthearted story for beginning readers about Timothy Trotter and his new dog. Tim is worried because Top does not bark. "Give him time," says the pet shop owner, and, at the right time, Top does bark.

The gay illustrations show that Timothy is brown-skinned and lives in an integrated neighborhood in a good residential section of a big city.

Fiction*

A book is a statue created by an author, or author and illustrator, to commemorate an idea, a passion, a condition, an event, an episode, a series of incidents, a feeling, a fact, a fancy, a memory, a search, an ideal, an individual and/or culture. Perhaps other things too. It is meant to be read and lived, rather than looked at, and in this it differs from many statues. But in other ways it is the same: it exists in time and space; it has shape, conformity and finiteness—it is a part of the world and not the whole; it is created with skill and craft, but these are aids to its development and not the purport of the work; it is an outward symbol of what it commemorates for the author, but what it expresses for others can be something quite different.

When the seeking mind of a child sees life below the surface of a book, pleasure, wonder, and sometimes a new process of creation begins. That is what children's books are for.

—George A. Woods

Bacmeister, Rhoda W. VOICES IN THE NIGHT. Bobbs, 1965. $3.25. 4–6

New England and an Underground Railroad station are the background for this story. When Jeanie's widowed mother is forced to break up her family because she cannot take care of them, Jeanie is sent to live with the Aldens, who secretly operate a station. The most important aspect of the book is the way in which a young person can become involved in an idea and movement which most adults would feel might be beyond her understanding. Jeanie saves the life of one runaway and helps with the wonderful Freedom Day celebration when the Emancipation Proclamation is issued. Although characterization is not especially well done, the story has a good pace, suspense, and details of everyday living.

Baker, Betty. WALK THE WORLD'S RIM. Harper, 1965. $2.95. (Library binding $2.95 net) Junior High

In Cabeza de Vaca's party searching for the gold of Cibola in the sixteenth century, there were three Spaniards and a giant Negro,

* See also Sports Fiction.

Esteban, who is the real hero of the book. The Indian boy who accompanies the party when it leaves for Mexico has come to idolize Esteban and hopes to grow up to be as capable and wise as he.

Poses universal problems which should provoke young people into thinking. Excellent writing style with simple construction and good characterization and dialogue.

BALL, DOROTHY WHITNEY. HURRICANE: THE STORY OF A FRIENDSHIP. Bobbs, 1964. $3.50. Paper (Grosset) $.50. Junior High

A story set in rural Florida today, the title incident occurs toward the end of the book and is of only minor importance. Davey lives alone with his grandfather (Pop) on a rather isolated farm; but, with a friend like Luke Washington, Davey is never lonely. Pop doesn't seem to think anything of the fact that Luke is a Negro until cousin Mike comes for a visit and comments with easy contempt on the friendship. Then Mike suggests that Luke is the person guilty of a knifing incident; Davy defends Luke, and it is discovered that Mike did the knifing himself. The rest of the story is episodic.

The writing style is adequate, the plot is weak, and the characterization is variable but good for the part; the book's strength is the objective picture of a rural southern community in which there is a range of reactions to the friendship.

BARRETT, WILLIAM E. LILIES OF THE FIELD. Illustrated. Doubleday, 1962. $2.95. Paper (Popular Library, 1963) $.40. Junior High

Homer Smith, driving cross country in his station wagon, stops to do a day's work in a southwestern valley where a group of German and Hungarian nuns are trying to establish a mission. Intrigued by their self-reliance, determination, and simplicity—as well as their total ignorance of the English language and the American "habit" of prejudice—he decides to stay with them a while. He secures a job, adds to their simple menu, and purchases a bathtub, while building a chapel for them. He refuses aid with the chapel until forced to accept it; he wants the edifice to be a product of his labor alone. He departs, leaving a legend.

This fast-moving story reads like a fable; it is sprinkled with humor and is believable. Easy vocabulary, simple concepts.

BAUM, BETTY. PATRICIA CROSSES TOWN. Illustrated. Knopf, 1965. $3.50. (Library binding $3.39 net) 4–6

Twelve-year-old Patricia is one of the first New York children to be bussed across town to integrate an all-white school. Impulsive and mischievous, she is suspicious of all white children and afraid of being rejected. Her teacher in the new school uses her interests in puppetry and acting to help her gain confidence; these interests also lead to her friendship with Sarah, who overcomes Pat's distrust. Sarah and another white girl later come across town to show their affection for Pat and put on their interracial puppet show to celebrate Pat's father's return from the hospital.

The writing is occasionally marred by artificial dialogue; a few of the illustrations are stereotypes.

BLANTON, CATHERINE. HOLD FAST TO YOUR DREAMS. Messner, 1955. $2.95. Junior High

Fifteen-year-old Emmy Lou wants to leave Blossom, Alabama, because of the restrictions placed on her as a member of an all-white dancing class. She wants to be a dancer more than anything; she hears there is no segregation in Mesa, Arizona, and leaves her father, a physician, and Granny, the woman who cares for her, and goes to Mesa for her last year in high school. Her aunt warns her not to expect too much even in Mesa. Emmy Lou experiences a series of disappointments: the guidance counselor refuses to permit her to join the advanced dancing class, telling her to be realistic; Emmy discovers that the Ballerinas (a dance club) is closed; she is given the lead in the school presentation, but the director takes it away two weeks before opening night. However, Emmy holds fast to her dreams, gets the lead in the Fiesta Ballet, and is admitted to the New York School of Theatre and Dance.

Features a romance between Emmy Lou and Dave Wallis, a Negro boy who wants to be a doctor. Will appeal to teenage readers.

BONHAM, FRANK. DURANGO STREET. Dutton, 1965. $3.75. Junior High

A starkly realistic and timely book about a southern California slum, somewhat like Watts and its people, although it is not about riots. It is about the poverty, the gangs, the hopelessness, the decay of the group, and the hope of an individual. Rufus Henry, a sixteen-year-old parolee from Pine Valley Camp, returns home to his fatherless family in a new neighborhood, a dilapidated duplicate of their former location. Rufus half-heartedly wishes that it were possible not to join a gang, but he knows that to stay alive in the "jungle" he must join a fighting gang. Within two days, Rufus has become embroiled in a fight with the Gassers, has quit his dirty, smelly job where his employer called him a "jailbird," has had a brutal initiation into the Moors, and is in trouble with the police again. Alex Robbins, a social worker, tries to reach Rufus through his hero worship of Ernie Brown, Cleveland Corsairs halfback. The book ends with a flicker of hope for him but leaves the problems unresolved and unfinished. Rufus is sympathetically portrayed, and Bonham has presented a contempory social problem forthrightly. A first of its kind.

BONTEMPS, ARNA. CHARIOT IN THE SKY: A STORY OF THE JUBILEE SINGERS. Illustrated by Cyrus Leroy Baldridge. Holt, 1951. Library binding, $3.27 net. (A Land of the Free book) Junior High

The dramatic story of Caleb Williams, born a slave, is the framework of this book, which also relates the early struggles of Fisk University and the founding of the Jubilee Singers.

Through Caleb's search for freedom and full manhood and the trials of the singers, Arna Bontemps presents the full impact of slavery and racial discrimination in a way rarely found in books for young people. His writing is a fine example of the difference between a phony dialect which depends mainly on exaggerated spelling, making it difficult to read, and the southern dialect in the hand of a skilled, knowledgeable craftsman.

BRINSMEAD, HESBA FAY. PASTURES OF THE BLUE CRANE. Coward, 1966. $3.95. 8 and up

A long junior novel set in Australia today, originally published in 1964, this book is patterned in its basic structure and most unusual in its development and variation. Basically, an orphan inherits a fortune and her life changes; she finds a grandfather of whom she knew nothing, and for the first time she puts down roots with a family, a home, and friends. The unusual aspect of the book is the slow unveiling to the reader of the fact that Ryl, the heroine, is of mixed blood and unaware of it. Her new friend Perry, who is a quartercaste, is clearly the most stable and charming of the new circle of friends; indeed, Perry is more relaxed when baited about his color than is Ryl herself. Perry is relaxed because he has self-respect and intelligence; it is surely due to his influence that Ryl adjusts so quickly to the fact that she has colored ancestry (Tongan) when she is finally told. The fact that Perry turns out to be Ryl's brother seems a bit contrived, but it is a minor weakness in a book with a good picture of rural Australia and a message of the innate worth of the individual.

BRODSKY, MIMI. THE HOUSE AT 12 ROSE STREET. Illustrated by David Hodges. Abelard, 1966. $3.50. 5–7

Bobby is delighted to have a boy his own age move into the house next door—and so is his family. Unfortunately, this is not true of all the residents of the suburban community where his family lives, because the Franklins are Negroes. He is attacked by a group of boys because he refuses to go along with their campaign of intimidation. The worst blow is the loss of his best friend, whose family is most opposed to integration.

The attempt to start a movement of panic selling is counteracted by good community organization. Will Franklin is finally accepted by the neighborhood boys and the Boy Scout troop. The problems are realistically handled, and it is good to have an example of a community where the adults play a leading role in helping to solve the acceptance of the first Negro family in an all-white community.

BURCH, ROBERT. QUEENIE PEAVY. Illustrated. Viking, 1966. $3.50. (Library binding $3.37 net) Junior High

A very good story of the depression era, set in a rural area. Queenie, an only child whose father is in jail and whose mother works, is a rebel and a hoyden. Queenie is shocked into a reassessment of herself when her father's return brings more trouble rather than the solution to all her problems as she had expected it would. One of the most pleasant facets of the story is in the relationship between Queenie and the two younger Corry children; they look up to her and she responds with a protective affection that is based on their affection, not their status. Indeed, the Corry family, which is Negro, is both more respectable and in better financial circumstances than is Queenie's family.

BURDEN, SHIRLEY. I WONDER WHY . . . Doubleday, 1963. $1.95. Junior High

In his note to this book, photographer Edward Steichen says, "In this poem of photographs and words, Shirley Burden has expressed a lovely child's wistful question that partakes of the holiness of prayer, and sears the conscience of us all."

The great impact of this book comes from its fine photographs and minimal text. The text catalogs the dear and universal loves of mankind—woods, snow at Christmas, clouds against a blue sky. The last picture, captioned "I wonder why some people don't like me," shows a Negro child's face, half-shadowed and deep in thought, wondering and wistful. This is an excellent book for stimulating discussion.

BUTTERS, DOROTHY G. MASQUERADE. Macrae, 1961. $3.50. Junior High

An honest and understanding story about Cora, a Negro girl who finds herself inadvertently passing as white, and her three dormitory mates. When the truth comes out, Cora is relieved and not at all surprised to be evicted from the school dormitory, but she is surprised that two of her friends are indignant and decide to share an apartment with her.

A sensitive and gratifying story for older girls.

CARLSON, NATALIE SAVAGE. THE EMPTY SCHOOLHOUSE. Illustrated by John Kaufmann. Harper, 1965. $3.95. (Library binding $3.79 net) 4–6

This award-winning story about a Negro family in a Louisiana parish is told by Emma, a fourteen-year-old school dropout. She is proud of her little sister Lullah, who is a bright student. Lullah and her best friend, who is white, look forward to going to the newly integrated St. Joseph's, but their joy is short-lived when violence is fomented by racists, and Lullah becomes the only pupil left in the school. Only after she is hurt in a racial incident do most of the parents of both groups feel shame and decide to send their children back to the school.

An honest, thoughtful, and timely book.

CAVANNA, BETTY. A TIME FOR TENDERNESS. Morrow, 1962. $3.50. Paper (Berkley) $.50. Junior High

Although the major portion of this teenage novel takes place in Brazil, we have included it on this list because it explores with honesty a "typical" American family's reaction to the lack of color prejudice in that country. Father, raised in New York, is accepting; Mother, a Southerner, is quite appalled, especially for the children; Tobey, the younger child, is without prejudice and manages to retain his integrity with a great deal of courage; and sixteen-year-old Peggy thinks she can see both sides. She is dismayed, however, when she learns that the aristocratic Carlos, with whom she has fallen in love, has a Negro grandmother. It is his family's social caste system which eventually keeps them apart.

CHANDLER, RUTH. LADDER TO THE SKY. Illustrated. Abelard, 1965. $3.50. 5–8

Chip Wood's family moves to a farm so his father, whose health was endangered by close office work, can raise nursery stock. Some families are friendly and some are not, but, when disaster strikes, this Negro family learns who their friends are. Although somewhat contrived, this is a warm story of growing up and friendship values.

CLARKE, MARY. PETTICOAT REBEL: SLAVE GIRL IN SCHOOL. Illustrated. Viking, 1964. $3.75. Junior High

A Revolutionary War story, set in Gloucester, Massachusetts. The rebel is Candace (Dacie) Tybott, sixteen years old and unashamedly hungry for more education than proper for a female. When the schoolmaster goes off to fight in the war, Candace is permitted to be a teacher—not only a teacher, but a teacher of girls! One of her pupils is Drusilla, a freed slave who was rescued after a shipwreck by Dacie's father; Mr. Tybott bought Drusilla and three men solely to set them free. The legality of their free status is questioned and cleared; Drusilla's suitor, Robin (an American Negro), is able to buy his freedom when he is given a reward for the capture of an American traitor. The three themes are very skillfully and smoothly woven together; the major theme is the introduction of education for girls, and the minor themes are those of slavery and of the relations and skirmishes with the British in the Gloucester area. As a period story with good historical background, this is both convincing and exciting; it is strengthened by the treatment of issues of social progress and is further strengthened by an objective attitude toward the British.

CLUFF, TOM. MINUTEMEN OF THE SEA. Illustrated by Tom O'Sullivan. Follett, 1955. $3.50. Junior High

A story about the little-known naval battle fought by the men of Machias Township, Maine, five days before Bunker Hill. This is a tightly-knit, swift-moving story about the Machias affair, but especially about the O'Brien clan and sixteen-year-old Joe O'Brien and Rebecca Moody, who play important and courageous roles.

One aspect of the story overlooked by reviewers is the natural inclusion of Dick Earl, a fugitive slave, who was hidden by Jeremiah O'Brien when he escaped from a schooner. The author's careful research brought to light not only the entire Machias affair but the role played by Dick, who by this time was considered a part of the O'Brien family and who emerges in this story as a heroic figure.

COBB, ALICE. THE SWIMMING POOL. Friendship, 1957. $2.50. (Paper $1.25; Study Guide $.50) 4–6

Although the message of this book is obtrusive, the story has value because of its elements of community interest, group action, friendship values, and intercultural understanding. Preston, a Negro boy, is not permitted to use a new swimming pool at Metropolis; Preston and his friend Benjy Weinberg decide to work for a new pool in their own community, a suburb of Metropolis. With a neighboring minister and a few other boys, they start to raise money and have a clean-up campaign. Community interest is aroused, and the whole community works together on the fund-raising project.

COLMAN, HILA. CLASSMATES BY REQUEST. Morrow, 1964. $3.50. Junior High

The problems of desegregating a high school are presented against a background of teenage romance, courageous parents, and children struggling with new attitudes. There are plans to boycott the segregated school, demonstrations, and picketing. Carla Monroe, whose father is active in city planning, is one of four white students who decide to attend the Negro school. Ten Negro students are transferred to the white school. Ella Randall, a Negro girl whose father has been active as an integrationist, is hostile to the change. Her unhappiness is climaxed when her father does not receive an engineering job for which he has applied. He is not qualified and understands, but Ella blames Carla's father since he could have made the recommendation. She refuses to discuss the issue with Carla, blaming it on prejudice. She is somewhat mollified when the city promises her friend, Eugene, a scholarship to a school of architecture.

These adolescent characters move in a real and serious world. Their romantic, political, and sociological problems are real and well explored. Doubts and fears receive as much discussion as courage. Difficult vocabulary and thought-provoking situations.

DE ANGELI, MARGUERITE. BRIGHT APRIL. Illustrated by the author. Doubleday, 1946. $3.50. 4–6

April Bright, a Negro Brownie Scout, helps her troop and a thoughtless member of the group toward understanding.

DE JONG, DOLA. ONE SUMMER'S SECRET. McKay, 1963. $3.00. Junior High

Seventeen-year-old Laurie is spending her vacation with her father at their summer home. Her attempt to help a Negro girl, who has run away from an unhappy foster home and is hiding in an empty cottage, leads to serious complications. To her relief, her father proves very understanding and helps her with the authorities. The Negro-white relationship is honest and logical. The story has excellent characterization and a good plot line.

DE LEEUW, ADÈLE. BARRED ROAD (rev. ed.). Macmillan, 1964. $3.00. (Library binding $3.74 net) Junior High

When Susan Trowbridge moves to a new town, she is shocked by the prejudice against Negro students in her high school. The classmate she admires most is Beth Varley, a gifted Negro girl. The Varleys move next door, to the dismay of Susan's mother. When Susan stands up for her beliefs, she antagonizes not only her school friends, but her boy friend and mother.

The growing friendship and maturity of both girls is well developed.

FALL, THOMAS. CANALBOAT TO FREEDOM. Illustrated by Joseph Cellini. Dial, 1966. $3.50. 6–8

This book describes a friendship between two boys, one a teenage orphan bound out on a canalboat and the other a Negro deckhand. The Negro protects the white boy from the cruelty of the captain, and the boy in turn joins the deckhand in his Underground Railroad activities.

FIFE, DALE. WHO'S IN CHARGE OF LINCOLN? Illustrated by Paul Galdone. Coward, 1965. $2.95. (Library binding $2.86 net) 3–5

Eight-year-old Lincoln's mother has made careful plans for him and his sisters for the time she is to be in the hospital. The baby, however, comes early, and Lincoln finds himself alone—with everyone thinking he is with the woman his mother hired. A thief dumps a bag of money in Lincoln's hands, and he decides that he will have to find his oldest sister in Washington, D.C. His train ride to Washington proves no problem; he leaves the money at the foot of the Lincoln statue, rides back to New York without finding his sister and without a ticket. Nobody will believe his story.

The tale is not as silly as outlined here because it is told in a matter-of-fact way, but third to fifth graders will enjoy reading it. A treatment of a middle-class Negro family in a large city; family relationships are excellent.

FRIERMOOD, ELIZABETH HAMILTON. WHISPERING WILLOWS. Doubleday, 1964. $3.50. Junior High

Although somewhat slow in pace, this is a fine period story of an orphaned girl who lives with her uncle, caretaker of a cemetery, in a small Indiana town in 1910. Tess is a tall girl who feels awkward and inadequate; she sees herself as an outsider. Her best friend is a Negro girl, and she feels almost a member of this warm, loving, and believable family. The position of the Washington family in a small town of the period is honestly drawn.

FRITZ, JEAN. BRADY. Illustrated by Lynd Ward. Coward, 1960. $3.50. 4–9

A story set in Pennsylvania in 1836. Although Brady Minton feels some embarrassment at his father's fervent feelings about slavery, he is sympathetic to the abolitionist position. As he gains enough responsibility to be trusted with information about the Underground Railroad, Brady finds that his opinions have strengthened.

The book has good period details and superb characterization. Some of the scenes give vivid pictures of community feeling: for example, one in which a slave catcher bullies a free Negro who is well liked in town and whose quiet besting of the other affords delight to the men standing about.

GATES, DORIS. LITTLE VIC. Illustrated by Kate Seredy. Viking, 1951. $3.50. (Library binding $3.37 net) 5–7

It isn't easy for a homeless Negro boy to win the right to ride the horses, and to race the son of Victory is not for an unknown groom. Although forbidden to ride, Pony Rivers rides Little Vic and saves some campers from a flash flood. Then he hitchhikes to Santa Anita and convinces Little Vic's owner that he can win the handicaps. Terse, short sentences keep the story moving until Pony overcomes his own handicap.

A moving story which will reach a wide audience of boys and girls because the hero is one with whom they can identify emotionally and admire for his determination and strength of character. One does not become aware of Pony's color until well into the story.

GRAHAM, LORENZ. NORTH TOWN. Crowell, 1965. $3.95. 6–9

David Williams and his family come north to escape bigotry and violence only to find in the industrial town where they now live that bigotry still exists, although in a more subtle form. David has a difficult time adjusting to an integrated high school, and the family faces a series of crises but finally can see a greater security than they had in the South.

A realistic picture which is not always pleasant but which gives an honest portrayal of conditions and holds out the hope of a better life.

————. SOUTH TOWN. Follett, 1958. $3.50. 6–9

Sixteen-year-old David Williams plans to go away to college to become a doctor and then return to his small town where doctors are so badly needed in the Negro community. His dreams are shattered when his father's independence is resented by a few influential white citizens who resort to violence to terrorize the family. For the sake of David's education, the family moves north.

This is an honest and moving story about the hopes and aspirations of people concerned with improving their opportunities.

HAAS, BEN. TROUBLED SUMMER. Bobbs, 1966. $4.00.

A gripping story of the effect of Klan violence in a sleepy little town in the Deep South. Clay Williams, a high-school senior, dreams of catching a huge bass to win the $500 prize which he wants to use for college. His plans are shattered when he accidentally finds the secret headquarters of the local Klan. He is badly beaten and warned to stay away from the river. This experience makes him bitter and deepens his distrust of all whites. When a group of civil rights workers come to help organize a rights drive, Clay cannot accept the white leader of the group. He withdraws inside himself, but he cannot stay away and finally becomes involved, spies on a Klan meeting, and, at the risk of his life, is able to save his uncle's church from bombing.

This gives a good picture of how a small community is organized into nonviolent movement and of the courage needed to stand up to violence without retaliating in kind. Included are the words to "We Shall Overcome," "If I Had a Hammer," and excerpts from other freedom songs. *Lions in the Way* by Bella Rodman has a similar theme.

HAYES, FLORENCE S. SKID. Illustrated by Elton C. Fax. Houghton, 1948. $3.25. 5–7

Skid moves from Georgia to a suburban community in Connecticut where he is the only Negro in the school. He faces the problems of any new boy in making a place for himself but earns the acceptance of students, teachers, and community. This is still popular, and children seem unconcerned by the few inaccuracies in the baseball plays.

HENTOFF, NAT. JAZZ COUNTRY. Harper, 1965. $3.50. (Library binding $3.27 net) 8 and up

An unusually fine, sophisticated novel of the contemporary jazz world in New York with a candid picture of racial attitudes. Sixteen-year-old Tom tries to make his way into a top-flight group of jazz musicians but learns that his life has been too easy and too limited for him to have something to say with his trumpet, even though his technique is good. It isn't an accident that most great jazz artists are Negroes! He perseveres, however, and learns much from the musicians he meets. Although his greatest desire is to play the trumpet, he decides that college should come first.

What has happened to him is best summarized by a friend who has watched him mature: "This last year has been a kind of trial for you, hasn't it? Trying to make it through the racial looking glass. Trying to make it in jazz. Trying to make it as a man . . . You've been trying very hard, Tom, to be, and not just exist."

For mature readers.

JUSTUS, MAY. NEW BOY IN SCHOOL. Illustrated by Joan Balfour Payne. Hastings, 1963. $2.95. 2–5

An integrated Tennessee school is the locale for this simply told story of a small Negro boy's adjustment in an all-white grade. His young parents suffer with him but are helpful and understanding.

————. A NEW HOME FOR BILLY. Illustrated by Joan Balfour Payne. Hastings, 1966. $3.25. (Library binding $3.03 net) 3–5

When his best friend is hurt playing in the street, Billy's father decides the family will leave the crowded apartment. After he finishes the painting job he has been working on, he and Billy drive out into the country. How they find a place to clean and paint and call home no matter what color their skin is a story one wishes would come true more often.

LEVY, MIMI COOPER. CORRIE AND THE YANKEE. Illustrated. Viking, 1959. $3.00. (Library binding $2.96 net) Junior High

An exciting story of Corrie, a ten-year-old slave girl, who hides a wounded Yankee soldier in her playhouse during the Civil War. She bravely guides him to the Union forces and is rewarded by finding her father, a scout in the northern army.

We have numerous stories in which the slave is helped by whites; this book presents a welcome contrast.

LEWIS, MARY. HALLOWEEN KANGAROO. Illustrated by Richard Lewis. Washburn, 1964. $2.95. (Library binding $2.92 net) 3–5

Jeffery wants to be a kangaroo at his school Halloween party, so his mother makes him a beautiful kangaroo costume. The story is about his misadventures with the zipper.

Illustrations show that Jeffery's family are Negroes and that his classmates are a very mixed group. The author-artist team are Negroes. For readers just beyond the beginning stage.

LEWIS, RICHARD W. A SUMMER ADVENTURE. Illustrated. Harper, 1962. $2.95. (Library binding $2.92 net) 3–5

A boy enjoys the woods and quarry about the farm, discovering animals and birds and one big turtle for his zoo. His father encourages his exploring, and slowly he learns of the balance in nature. The pictures show Ross as a Negro boy, and any boy who loves the outdoors will share in his adventures.

MAGEE, CATHERINE F. ONE OF THE FAMILY. McKay, 1964. $3.95. 8 and up

The story of a family into which a mongoloid baby is born. Against the advice of the doctor, the family brings Larry Joe home. His sister, Sally, is a college freshman; although she was at first embarrassed just by the fact that her mother was having a baby, it is she who insists that retarded children are educable. In the course of her school year, Sally also fights for integration in her sorority. The story is weakened by too many characters and by an inordinate amount of information presented as dialogue.

MARSHALL, CATHERINE. JULIE'S HERITAGE. McKay, 1957. $3.95. Paper (Scholastic) $.50. 6 and up

Julie Brownell, daughter of a Negro doctor, discovers now that she is entering senior high her two white friends, Doris and Betts, have deserted her. Hurt and bitter, she is sustained by a small group of boys and girls of her own race and by her driving ambition to be a singer. Her audition at Juilliard marks her first step toward fulfillment.

A credible book with real problems and possible, though rather simplified, solutions.

MEADOWCROFT, ENID L. BY SECRET RAILWAY. Illustrated. Crowell, 1948. $4.50. Paper (Scholastic, 1963) $.50. 5–7

Jim, a freed slave boy whose freedom depends on the certificate he keeps in his pocket, seeks shelter with David Morgan, a friendly white boy, in Chicago, 1860. The Morgans take in a boarder, who betrays Jim and kidnaps him in order to get the reward for runaway slaves. Then David sets out to find Jim and set him on his way to Canada by the Underground Railroad. The latter, nineteenth-century Chicago, and Lincoln's election campaign form the historical background.

An idealized story with oversimplified good and evil, but with enough adventure to keep a boy's interest. The analytical student might question the contrived plot, however, and Jim's speech is hardly in character.

MEANS, FLORENCE CRANNELL. REACH FOR A STAR. Illustrated. Houghton, 1957. $3.25. Junior High

A teenage novel about the daughter of a Denver dentist who goes to Fisk University where she makes new friends, experiences the discrimination of the South, and begins to find new directions for her own life. A well-rounded picture of Negro life at an economic and social level not often presented in books for young people.

NEWELL, HOPE H. A CAP FOR MARY ELLIS. Harper, 1952. $3.50. (Library binding $3.27 net) Junior High

Two Negro girls have the chance to attend an all-white nurses' training school after their high school graduation. Warned that they will be "pioneers," the girls decide to accept the challenge; their experiences are realistic, and the outcome is heartwarming.

In *Mary Ellis, Student Nurse* (1958), the adventures of the girls are continued.

PALMER, CANDIDA. SNOW STORM BEFORE CHRISTMAS. Illustrated by H. Tom Hall. Lippincott, 1965. $2.75. (Library binding $2.69 net) 3–5

A brief story about two brothers who are caught in a snowstorm when they go shopping on Christmas Eve. They ingeniously salvage their ruined presents, and the next morning they are able to enjoy the sights and scents of Christmas before joining the family.

The illustrations show an attractive middle-class Negro family.

RODMAN, BELLA. LIONS IN THE WAY. Follett, 1966. $3.95. (Library binding $3.96) Junior High

A story about high school integration in a Tennessee town, Jameson, which fought the Supreme Court decision for two years. Eight students from a Negro school have been chosen to attend Fayette, and trouble is fomented by an outside agitator who establishes a "white crusade," arousing the suppressed hostility of the town. Two of the eight youngsters give up; after some rioting in which a white minister is injured, the U.S. Army is called, and order is established. The fulcrum of action in the story is the minister, who moves from polite aloofness to impassioned involvement.

SHOTWELL, LOUISA R. ROOSEVELT GRADY. Illustrated by Peter Burchard. World, 1963. $2.95. (Library binding $2.88 net) Paper (Grosset, 1964) $.50. 5 and up

For nine-year-old Roosevelt Grady, son of migratory workers, the meaninglessness of life is symbolized in the Opportunity Class ("Please, Ma'am, opportunity for what?") and in the mathematics exercises which are always "taking away" but never "putting into." Roosevelt's dream of finding a permanent home becomes a reality when a friend, a few years older, helps him compose a letter inquiring about a job.

This is a warm, credible story, not unduly sentimental. Family relationships are realistic. Although some events in the lives of the migrant family may not be familiar, children in both urban and suburban communities will understand and sympathize with their hopes and dreams for a permanent home. Only the illustrations indicate that the hero is Negro.

SPRAGUE, GRETCHEN. A QUESTION OF HARMONY. Dodd, 1965. $3.25. Junior High

At a summer party, Jeanne meets an attractive boy from another high school; they find that they are both music lovers and performers; Jeanne plays cello, Dave piano. When Dave introduces his friend Mel, a violinist, a trio is born. The three stop for a snack one night after a performance and, because of Mel's presence, are refused service. This is Jeanne's introduction to real racial prejudice. Her education continues; for example, her best friend's mother snubs Dave when she finds out that he is Mel's friend. The owner of the hotel writes a note of apology after some critical newspaper publicity. When Mel wins first prize in a music contest, the manager who turned him away adds a large check. Mel finds it hard to accept this hypocrisy, but Dave's father points out that, however ignorant Jeanne may have been, both Dave and Mel knew that they were inviting a showdown at the restaurant. The attitudes and changes of attitudes are all believably drawn; the ending is satisfying without being pat.

Notable for its inclusion of an interest in classical music.

STERLING, DOROTHY. MARY JANE. Illustrated by Ernest Crichlow. Doubleday, 1959. Library binding $3.27 net. Paper (Scholastic, 1963) $.35. 5–8

Attending Wilson High School, Mary Jane discovers, is one of the most difficult experiences of her life—for she is the first Negro to be enrolled there. Loneliness is the most painful part of the experience. Compassion for a squirrel establishes communication between Mary Jane and Sally which develops into a strong and lasting friendship.

One of the first books to deal with school integration, this book still has a powerful emotional impact on the reader.

STOLZ, MARY. WHO WANTS MUSIC ON MONDAY? Harper, 1963. $3.95. (Library binding $3.79 net) 7 and up

A moving and intelligent book, perceptive in its analysis of family relationships, candid in its appraisal of race relations, true in its characterization and dialogue. Cass, an intelligent and fiercely honest girl of fourteen, is baffled by her older sister Lotta, a flirt. Mother is vaguely unhappy, vaguely bothered by Cassie's "oddness," and totally lacking in understanding of Vincent, the oldest, who is away at college.

Vincent's life at college is tied to the book only by back references and reactions to letters; he lives with an English boy and a southern Negro, and the three roommates are candid and compatible. The college year ends with an afternoon by the river: Vincent, David, and Vincent's love. David is bitter about the "inexorable penalty he would pay for that color all his life." But David, too, is young and in love; like the others, he has an unquenchable optimism.

WEIK, MARY HAYS. THE JAZZ MAN. Illustrated. Atheneum, 1966. $3.50. (Library binding $3.41 net) 5 and up

A harsh story of Zeke, a sensitive, crippled nine-year-old abandoned for a time by his parents in a fourth-floor Harlem apartment. His mother works; his father's jobs are uncertain and he drinks. Zeke does not go to school because he does not want to be teased about his lameness. His mother, discouraged by her husband's inability to support them, leaves, and father and son struggle along until finally father, too, leaves.

Lonely, hungry, and sick, Zeke listens to the jazz man playing the piano across the way. In a feverish dream, he imagines he visits the jazz man and is welcomed by lights, warmth, food, music, and laughter. He awakens to see his reunited parents, and it is hard for him to believe that he is not alone any more.

This book must be used with discrimination, particularly with young readers, since it deals so realistically with the devastating effect of poverty and abandonment. For the child who is secure in his home, this will give meaning to what he often sees on television or reads in the papers. For the child to whom this kind of situation is only too familiar, the book may be disturbing. The haunting woodcut illustrations add to the story's poignancy.

WHITNEY, PHYLLIS A. WILLOW HILL. McKay, 1947. Library binding $3.89 net. Junior High

The community of Willow Hill must face the issue of racial discrimination when Negroes move into the project at the foot of Willow Hill and are eligible to attend the neighborhood high school. Presented in this story are high school youngsters, such as eager Judy; her liberal friend Steve; her best friend Val, who is reluctant to be involved in the conflict; and Val's prejudiced friend, Tony. Parents' attitudes are also shown. Two Negro students help to effect a better understanding between the races.

An unsentimental study in race relations, both realistic and hopeful. Even though the immediate problems are solved, the author makes no pretense that problems in race relations are easily and quickly solved.

WIER, ESTER. EASY DOES IT. Illustrated by W. T. Mars. Vanguard, 1965. $3.50. 5–7

When Chip Woodman is eleven years old, his family moves into a new neighborhood. His interest in baseball helps him to make new friends. However, when a Negro boy moves next door, he is accepted by no one but Chip. The two become good friends, and Chip enjoys going to the Reeses' home. The latter are subjected to threats and a silent boycott. Chip's parents do not attend the protest meeting, but his mother is confused and finds it difficult to go against popular opinion. Finally, another meeting is held in Chip's home, and it is he who shames the adults into behaving decently.

Although some of the incidents seem contrived, on the whole the story is realistic, constructive, and easy to read.

WOODY, REGINA. ALMENA'S DOGS. Illustrated. Farrar, 1954. $3.50. (Ariel books) 4–6

Almena, an eleven-year-old Negro girl, wants a dog more than anything, but she lives in a New York apartment house where pets are forbidden. Fired by her desire to be a veterinarian, Almena devotes her spare time to taking care of other people's pets. Then her father has orders to open the stables at Sandy-Hill, a country estate which houses a large dog kennel. The story ends happily, for Almena will now live with her family on the estate and help care for the dogs.

The setting is urban and realistic; characters are believable. The story also has an interesting school background.

History

A race is like a man. Until it uses its own talents, takes pride in its own history, and loves its own memories it can never fulfill itself completely.

—JOHN W. VANDERCOOK

ACHESON, PATRICIA C. THE SUPREME COURT: AMERICA'S JUDICIAL HERITAGE. Dodd, 1961. $3.75. Junior High

A long and serious book in which the author thoroughly examines the role of the Supreme Court in American history, surveys the political and economic origins of some of the cases the court has decided, and evaluates the impact of those cases. Three chapters are concerned with the Negro in America. The first is a detailed and critical discussion of the Dred Scott decision and of the legislation and the conflicting points of view that preceded the debate, litigation, and decision. The second is an intensive examination of actions of the court during the years of the Civil War and the reconstruction period; to a lesser extent the chapter following, "The Big Business Years," is pertinent. A third chapter of vital interest is entitled "Our Constitution Is Color Blind." Here the discussion of legislation, court decisions, debate, review, and principles all pertain to segregation and the fight for equality and civil rights. Appended material includes a list of judges of the Supreme Court, a list of sources for cases cited in the text, an index, and the U.S. Constitution.

ANGELL, PAULINE K. TO THE TOP OF THE WORLD. Illustrated with maps and photographs. Rand, 1964. $4.50 Junior High

An account of the twenty-eight years devoted to reaching the North Pole by explorers Robert E. Peary and Matthew Henson, a Negro.

BONTEMPS, ARNA. ONE HUNDRED YEARS OF NEGRO FREEDOM. Illustrated. Dodd, 1961. $4.25. 7 and up

Arna Bontemps records the struggle of the Negro from the Emancipation Proclamation to Martin Luther King and the civil rights movement, through the personalities of educators, editors, scientists, politicians, and artists who played a part. All these are leaders in their fields, such as Booker T. Washington, Dr. William DuBois, Pinckney Pinchback, Theodore Greene, T. Motley Fortune, George Washington Carver, Emmett Scott, Paul Laurence Dunbar, and Charles S. Johnson, who furthered the advance of the American Negro.

————. STORY OF THE NEGRO (3rd ed.). Illustrated by Raymond Lufkin. Knopf, 1958. Library binding $3.69 net. 7 and up

A readable, dramatic, and accurate history of the Negro from his beginnings in Africa up to the present day. The historical events and the long struggle for freedom are made even more dramatic by the inclusion of the lives of people, Negro and white, who have played courageous and important roles in every area of life to forward the Negro's march toward complete integration.

BOWEN, DAVID. THE STRUGGLE WITHIN: RACE RELATIONS IN THE UNITED STATES. Norton, 1965. $3.50. (Library binding $3.28 net) 7 and up

In his preface, the author says, "There is no problem on which it is harder for the average person to find out exactly what the issues are, how they grew, and what Americans truly think about them. Most of us are not even sure why we hold the opinions we do." Then he proceeds in a frank and carefully researched book to examine all aspects of Negro-white relationships—the Negro's attitude about himself and the wide range of attitudes in both groups.

An informal, impartial, and unsentimental introduction for young people, which includes the discussion of the scientific information available on racial differences: economic causes and results of slavery and segregation, the psychological problems involved, and the difference between desegregation and integration. He ends with a hopeful look at the future. An index is appended.

BUCKMASTER, HENRIETTA. FLIGHT TO FREEDOM: THE STORY OF THE UNDERGROUND RAILROAD. Crowell, 1958. $3.95. 7 and up

An excellent history of the founding and operation of the Underground Railroad, with background material on slavery, the growth of the abolition movement in spite of opposition in the North, the leaders of both races, and the role of the Negro after the Civil War. Includes many accounts of the experiences of escaping slaves.

Bibliography appended.

DURHAM, PHILIP, and EVERETT L. JONES. THE ADVENTURES OF THE NEGRO COWBOYS. Dodd, 1965. $3.50. 6–9

Adapted from the adult book *The Negro Cowboys* for juvenile readers. Thrilling episodes of Broncho Sam, One-Horse Charley, and other colorful figures not found in any of the regular history books. Information is presented well; the treatment will inspire and enlighten the slow teenage reader. A useful book for older boys as history and enrichment material on this little-known subject.

FOSTER, G. ALLEN. THE EYES AND EARS OF THE CIVIL WAR. Illustrated with documentary photographs and engravings. Criterion, 1963. $3.95. 7 and up

Negro barbers, bartenders, and waiters listened and reported to northern generals or copied maps from tablecloths. Generals such as McClellan refused to believe in their intelligence; but Pinkerton discovered the freed slave, John Scobell, who became ostensibly an entertainer but actually a spy in the Confederate camp. Old Ben was sent by Sheridan to sell vegetables to Rebecca Wright, a Quaker, and carried messages back and forth, wrapped in foil in a decayed tooth.

GOLDMAN, PETER. CIVIL RIGHTS: THE CHALLENGE OF THE FOURTEENTH AMENDMENT. Coward, 1965. $3.25. (Challenge books) Junior High

A treatment of the history of the Negro in the United States, adequately illustrated by photographs and emphasizing the sharply accelerated struggle of the recent past. The writing is occasionally florid journalese, occasionally fictionalized, but fairly competent and never inaccurate. An inadequate bibliography (many good recent books omitted and some mediocre sports biographies cited) and an index are appended; the words and music of "We Shall Overcome" are printed at both the beginning and the end of the book.

HUGHES, LANGSTON, and MILTON MELTZER. PICTORIAL HISTORY OF THE NEGRO IN AMERICA (rev. ed.). Illustrated with maps. Crown, 1963. $5.95. Junior High

A panoramic history of the Negro in the United States. Excellent, concise text and numerous old prints, engravings, woodcuts, and photographs.

JOHNSTON, JOHANNA. TOGETHER IN AMERICA: THE STORY OF TWO RACES AND ONE NATION. Illustrated. Dodd, 1965. $3.50. 5–8

Although far from comprehensive, this is an adequate history of the Negro people in the United States from the days of the slave trade to the passage of the civil rights law. Unfortunately, the text skips in continuity from 1909 to 1963. The writing style is excellent; the bibliography is not up-to-date; an index is appended.

MCCARTHY, AGNES, and LAWRENCE REDDICK. WORTH FIGHTING FOR: A HISTORY OF THE NEGRO IN THE UNITED STATES DURING THE CIVIL WAR AND RECONSTRUCTION. Illustrated. Doubleday, 1965. $2.95. (Zenith books) Paper $1.45. 6–9

One of a series about minority groups in the United States. The writing style is very staid, the material dramatic and useful—despite the approach—as a background for understanding the problems of today.

MCPHERSON, JAMES M. THE NEGRO'S CIVIL WAR: HOW NEGROES FELT AND ACTED DURING THE WAR FOR THE UNION. Pantheon, 1965. $6.95. Junior High

The author presents documentary evidence from Negro and abolitionist newspapers, pamphlets, letters, speeches, and official records to show that Negroes actively participated and many became leaders in the emancipation of the slaves from 1860 to 1865.

An impressive history of the Negro's contribution both on the battlefields of the war and in civilian life; a good source book for the teacher.

MELTZER, MILTON, ed. IN THEIR OWN WORDS: A HISTORY OF THE AMERICAN NEGRO. 2 vols., 1619–1865, 1865–1916. Illustrated with contemporary engravings and facsimiles. Crowell, 1964 (Vol. I), 1965 (Vol. II). $4.95 each. 7 and up

A dramatic, moving, and unique history of the American Negro told in his own words through selections from letters, diaries, journals, autobiographies, speeches, resolutions, newspapers, and pamphlets. Each selection is introduced briefly, and the material is arranged from slavery to Emancipation and the close of the Civil War, through 1916. Some of the documents are given in full; many are abridged. Also includes a calendar of Negro history, an annotated reading list, and an index. An invaluable source book for teachers.

————, and AUGUST MEIER. TIME OF TRIAL, TIME OF HOPE: THE NEGRO IN AMERICA, 1919–1941. Illustrated by Moneta Barnett. Doubleday, 1966. $2.95. (Zenith books) Paper $1.45 Junior High

A clear and objective account, beginning with the return of the Negro soldier from World War I and ending with the threat of a march on Washington. The march was prevented by the establishment of the first Fair Employment Practices Commission, for which A. Philip Randolph fought. There are few books which deal with this period in the Negroes' struggle for economic survival and against court injustices and lynching.

MIERS, EARL SCHENCK. THE STORY OF THE AMERICAN NEGRO. Illustrated with photographs. Grosset, 1965. $1.95. (Library binding $2.39 net; paper .69) Junior High

The author has divided his subject into three revolutions: the American Revolution, which freed the colonists from political domination; the Civil War, which freed the Negro from legal domination; and the present Negro revolution to free him from social domination. This broad view is bolstered by quotations from many sources and photographs.

SCHECTER, BETTY. THE PEACEABLE REVOLUTION. Illustrated. Houghton, 1963. $3.75. 8 and up

A book about nonviolent resistance. The first and shortest section discusses Thoreau and "Civil Disobedience"; the second is a biography of Gandhi, emphasizing his advocation of peaceful resistance. The third describes the various patterns of nonviolent resistance in the United

States today, including the Montgomery bus boycott, sit-ins, and freedom rides.

SPANGLER, EARL. THE NEGRO IN AMERICA. Lerner, 1966. $3.79.

A superficial treatment of Negro history in the United States, profusely illustrated with photographs and reproductions of old prints. Much of the material is interesting, and the text as a whole is informative, but the book is weakened by random arrangement, lack of an index, and emphasis on great numbers of people discussed rather than in-depth studies.

STERLING, DOROTHY. FOREVER FREE: THE STORY OF THE EMANCIPATION PROCLAMATION. Illustrated by Ernest Crichlow. Doubleday, 1963. $3.50. 7 and up

A comprehensive, well-documented, and vivid history of slavery in the United States—North and South—told against the background of other events. Includes lesser-known heroes as well as the famous fighters in the abolition movement and the Negro's struggle for freedom. The book closes when the Emancipation Proclamation is issued.

Includes a long list of source materials and a full index, which shows quoted materials by italics.

————. TENDER WARRIORS. Illustrated with photographs. Hill, 1958. Junior High

As the three photographs on the front cover reveal, this is, essentially, an account of young people, Negro and white, caught up in one of the major conflicts of our generation—the struggle to integrate the southern school. The reporter visited the homes and talked with the "tender warriors," who survived both emotional and physical hurts. Aided by realistic photographs of what really happened in Little Rock and by vivid accounts of how people felt about what was happening, the book tells the story honestly.

Its high interest level should make it possible for slower readers, and its theme and concepts are compelling enough for more advanced readers.

STERNE, EMMA GELDERS. I HAVE A DREAM. Illustrated by Tracy Sugarman. Knopf, 1965. $3.95. (Library binding $3.39 net) 7 and up

A stirring book which tells the story of the civil rights movement today through the biographies of nine people who have played prominent roles. Well-organized material links the separate sections together so that this is much more than a collection of biographies.

YOUNG, MARGARET B. THE FIRST BOOK OF AMERICAN NEGROES. Watts, 1966. $2.65. (Library binding $1.98 net)

A history of the Negro in the United States, with emphasis on the civil rights issues of today and the historical patterns that have led to them. The text is topically arranged by education, employment, etc.; within each section the arrangement is roughly chronological. The text has considerable lapses of syntax but on the whole is fairly well written. The sections on sports and theater are studded with names of well-known contemporary figures, while the historical sections seldom give individual names; it seems odd, nevertheless, to find Jimmy Brown and Sammy Davis cited in the index, but neither Mary McLeod Bethune nor George Washington Carver.

Biography

Children can identify with all things and all creatures. Brotherhood is natural to them. If, then, we foster and preserve and mature this empathy, the men and women they become will be able to project themselves into the hearts and minds of other people. They will be able to know the people of the earth by sharing their being. Then, I think, we can build; we can really achieve that ultimate good, "peace on earth."

—ELIZABETH BORTON DE TREVINO

Collective Biography

ADAMS, RUSSELL L. GREAT NEGROES: PAST AND PRESENT (2nd ed.). Edited by David P. Ross, Jr. Illustrated by Eugene Winslow. Afro-American, 1964. $5.95.

Short biographies of over 150 outstanding Negroes. Illustrations, source notes, and an extensive bibliography add to the book's value. Arranged according to field of endeavor.

A useful reference book for the home and large libraries that have other, more extensive reference books.

ANGELL, PAULINE K. TO THE TOP OF THE WORLD. Illustrated with maps and photographs. Rand, 1964. $4.50. Junior High

This biography of two men, explorers Robert E. Peary and Matthew Henson, a Negro, gives an account of the twenty-eight years Peary and Henson devoted to reaching the North Pole. The author corrects the impression that Henson continued his original role as Peary's body servant by showing that he was an indispensable assistant in the scientific aspect of the expeditions.

Exciting as a fictional adventure story; informative as a historical account of Arctic explorations.

BONTEMPS, ARNA. FAMOUS NEGRO ATHLETES. Illustrated with photographs. Dodd, 1964. $3.50. Junior High

Biographical sketches of Joe Louis, Sugar Ray Robinson, Jackie Robinson, Satchel Paige, Willie Mays, Jesse Owens, Wilt Chamberlain, Jim Brown, and Althea Gibson. Although the emphasis is on sports achievements, the author does give an account of their personal lives. A popular collection.

————. ONE HUNDRED YEARS OF NEGRO FREEDOM. Illustrated. Dodd, 1961. $4.25. Junior High

Historical treatment of contributors to Negro progress; includes such leaders in their fields as Booker T. Washington, Dr. William DuBois, Pinckney Pinchback, Theodore Greene, T. Motley Fortune, George Washington Carver, Emmett Scott, Paul Laurence Dunbar, and Charles S. Johnson.

DOBLER, LAVINIA G., and EDGAR A. TOPPIN. PIONEERS AND PATRIOTS: LIVES OF SIX NEGROES OF THE REVOLUTIONARY ERA. Illustrated by Colleen Browning. Doubleday, 1965. $2.95. (Paper $1.45) Junior High

Selected as representative of a variety of contributions to America are Peter Salem, who shot a British leader at Bunker Hill; Jean Baptiste du Sable, who chose the Chicago site for his trading post; Phillis Wheatley, the poet; Benjamin Banneker, astronomer and almanac compiler; Paul Cuffee, navigator; John Chavis, preacher and teacher. The accounts are short, dignified narratives relating abilities and equality of early American Negroes in many walks of life, the last four requiring considerable intellectual ability.

DOUTY, ESTHER M. UNDER THE NEW ROOF: FIVE PATRIOTS OF THE YOUNG REPUBLIC. Illustrated with portraits. Rand, 1965. $4.50. 4–6

This biography of five American patriots includes a Negro, Richard Allen, founder of the African Methodist Episcopal Church. This humble churchman distinguished himself as a great humanitarian during the yellow fever epidemic of 1793. He was also one of the Negroes who took an active part in the War of 1812. His is a little-known but important contribution to early American history.

HUGHES, LANGSTON. FAMOUS AMERICAN NEGROES. Illustrated. Dodd, 1954. $3.50. 5 and up

This collection of short biographies covers a period of two hundred years, beginning with the story of Phillis Wheatley, poet of Colonial times, and concluding with the life of Jackie Robinson, first Negro in major league baseball. A wide variety of careers and personalities is included. Interestingly presented; informative.

————. FAMOUS NEGRO HEROES OF AMERICA. Illustrated. Dodd, 1958. $3.50. 5 and up

In interesting biographical sketches, Hughes tells of contributions sixteen Negroes have made to America. Some of the personalities included are warriors, pioneers, abolitionists, and seamen, such as Estaban, credited with the discovery of what is now Arizona; Crispus Attucks, first to die for American independence; Jean Baptiste Pointe du Sable, founder of Chicago; and Ida B. Wells, crusader. Spans a period from the founding of the nation through World War II.

The author includes figures not found in his *Famous American Negroes.*

————. FAMOUS NEGRO MUSIC MAKERS. Illustrated. Dodd, 1955. $3.50. 6–10

Short biographies of seventeen outstanding Negro musicians, including James A. Bland, Dean Dixon, Bill Robinson, "Leadbelly," William Grant Still, Fisk Jubilee Singers, Bert Williams, Jelly Roll Morton, Roland Hayes, Bessie Smith, Duke Ellington, Ethel Waters, Louis Armstrong, Marian Anderson, Bennie Benjamin, Mahalia Jackson, and Lena Horne.

NATHAN, DOROTHY. WOMEN OF COURAGE. Illustrated by Carolyn Cather. Random, 1964. $1.95. (Library binding $2.28 net) (Landmark books) 5–8

The women are Susan B. Anthony, Jane Addams, Mary McLeod Bethune, Amelia Earhart, and Margaret Mead, all of whom "stand out for their boldness and imagination." Mary McLeod Bethune's eventful life and accomplishments will interest readers.

RICHARDSON, BEN. GREAT AMERICAN NEGROES. Revised by William A. Fahey. Illustrated by Robert Hallock. Crowell, 1956. $4.50. 6 and up

This collection, originally published in 1945, has been brought up to date, and new material has been added. Twenty-six people are now included who have made a significant contribution to American life. The lives are arranged under the headings of music, the theatre, art, literature, education, the church, civic leadership, science, sports, and the military. There is an index.

ROLLINS, CHARLEMAE HILL. FAMOUS AMERICAN NEGRO POETS. Dodd, 1965. $3.95. Junior High

A collective biography of twelve Negro poets, their inclusion based on their appeal to the young reader. Each brief sketch includes some material about the writer's personal life and some about his literary contribution, with a quotation included. Some other significant poets are mentioned in the preface. Includes a bibliography and an index.

————. THEY SHOWED THE WAY: FORTY AMERICAN NEGRO LEADERS. Crowell, 1964. $3.00. 5–8

Each sketch is only a few pages long; the subjects are not living, so that many of the familiar names of our time are not included. Some of the subjects made minor contributions, and others are pioneers in their fields.

STERLING, DOROTHY, and BENJAMIN QUARLES. LIFT EVERY VOICE. Illustrated by Ernest Crichlow. Doubleday, 1965. $2.95. (Zenith books) (Paper $1.45) Junior High

Well-told, objective, and straightforward accounts of the lives of Booker T. Washington, William E. B. DuBois, Mary Church Terrell, and James Weldon Johnson. Booker T. Washington is the best known of the four. William E. B. DuBois, a leading Negro historian, founded the NAACP. Mrs. Terrell, a graduate of Oberlin College, was the wife of the first Negro federal judge. She not only fought for the equality of the Negro but also participated in the suffragist cause and the peace movement under Jane Addams. James Weldon Johnson was a poet, teacher, lawyer, editor of the first Negro newspaper, and diplomatic consul under Theodore Roosevelt.

The authors have successfully integrated into each biography the ways in which the paths of the four crossed. Indexed.

STERNE, EMMA GELDERS. BLOOD BROTHERS: FOUR MEN OF SCIENCE. Illustrated by Oscar Liebman. Knopf, 1959. $3.00. 5–8

Dramatic biographies of four scientists whose discoveries enlarged our knowledge of blood. Includes Dr. Charles Drew, the Negro scientist who was first to find the method for processing raw blood into plasma available for instant transfusions.

————. I HAVE A DREAM. Illustrated by Tracy Sugarman. Knopf, 1965. $3.95. (Library binding $3.39 net) 7 and up

A stirring book which tells the story of the civil rights struggle today through the biographies of nine people who have played prominent roles. Well-organized material links the separate sections together, so that this is much more than a collection of individual biographies. The leaders come from a wide area of interests; included are Marian Anderson, A. Philip Randolph, James Farmer, John Lewis, Thurgood Marshall, Hugh Mulzac, Rosa Lee Parks, and Fred Shuttleworth.

An excellent bibliography and index are appended.

STRATTON, MADELINE. NEGROES WHO HELPED BUILD AMERICA. Illustrated. Ginn, 1965. $2.80. Junior High

Short biographies of Abbott, Anderson, Bethune, Bunche, Davis, Douglass, Drew, DuBois, Julian, King, Robinson, Washington, Williams, and Woodson. Interest is expanded by general discussions of an entire area; for example, Negro artists are discussed in an introduction preceding the biography of Marian Anderson.

The photographs are good, but the other illustrations add little information. The straightforward writing will make this useful with slow readers, and younger children can use it for limited reference.

TERKEL, LOUIS (STUDS). GIANTS OF JAZZ. Illustrated. Crowell, 1957. $3.50. Junior High

A collective biography that describes twelve jazz artists. The writing style is informal, the emphasis on each musician's contribution to the development of jazz. Many of the artists discussed are Negro; there are many references in the text to minor jazz luminaries.

Individual Biographies and Autobiographies*

Louis Armstrong

EATON, JEANETTE. TRUMPETER'S TALE: THE STORY OF YOUNG LOUIS ARMSTRONG. Illustrated. Morrow, 1955. $3.95. Junior High

A warm, honest biography, almost as interesting a chapter in the history of jazz as it is a picture of one of the great men of jazz. The author candidly describes Armstrong's childhood in a slum and his removal from a detention home to the Colored Waifs' Home. The years as a musician on the road are vividly described; the ebullient personality is so sympathetically drawn that Armstrong's success and fame come as a satisfying conclusion. The illustrations are of poor calibre; dialect is used throughout the book.

Crispus Attucks

MILLENDER, DHARATHULA H. CRISPUS ATTUCKS: BOY OF VALOR. Bobbs, 1965. $2.25. (Text ed. $1.96) (Childhood of Famous Americans series) 3–5

This is a story of the early childhood and later life of the man who on March 5, 1770, was shot and killed by British soldiers in the struggle for American independence. Although little is known of Crispus Attucks, a Negro who was among the first to give his life in the cause of freedom, this is an inspiring story for younger children.

Benjamin Banneker

GRAHAM, SHIRLEY. YOUR MOST HUMBLE SERVANT: THE STORY OF BENJAMIN BANNEKER. Messner, 1949. $3.50. (Library binding $3.34 net) Junior High

A detailed and inspiring account of the eighteenth century Negro mathematician, inventor, architect, scholar, and planner of the nation's capitol.

Mary McLeod Bethune

PEARE, CATHERINE OWENS. MARY MC LEOD BETHUNE. Vanguard, 1951. $3.95. Junior High

In this excellent biography of one of America's great women, the emphasis is on Mrs. Bethune's contribution to the improvement of education for the Negro in the South and the establishment of Bethune-Cookman College in Florida.

STERNE, EMMA GELDERS. MARY MC LEOD BETHUNE. Illustrated by Raymond Lufkin. Knopf, 1957. $3.50. (Library binding $3.79 net) Junior High

* See also Sports Biographies.

A sympathetic and absorbing biography of the remarkable Negro educator, who served in many capacities: in the National Youth administration under Franklin Delano Roosevelt, as consultant in framing the Charter for the Declaration of Human Rights for the United Nations, in women's rights, etc.

Ralph J. Bunche

KUGELMASS, J. ALVIN. RALPH J. BUNCHE: FIGHTER FOR PEACE (rev. ed.). Messner, 1962. $3.25. (Library binding $3.19 net) Junior High

Kugelmass introduces this biography with a discussion of the slave era and with information about Bunche's ancestry. He tells of Bunche's poverty-ridden childhood in Detroit and how, despite being orphaned and impoverished, this onetime newspaper and shoeshine boy was graduated from UCLA with honors. He began a career that won for him perhaps the longest string of university degrees in American history and the Nobel Peace Prize.

This storylike, poetic account also tells of Bunche as a human being interested in young people and their problems. Will appeal to readers of all levels. Highly recommended.

George Washington Carver

ALIKI (Aliki Brandenberg). A WEED IS A FLOWER: THE LIFE OF GEORGE WASHINGTON CARVER. Illustrated by the author. Prentice, 1965. $4.25. K–3

A read-aloud picturebook biography. Writing style is rather stilted but adequate; coverage is light but fairly well balanced.

COY, HAROLD. THE REAL BOOK ABOUT GEORGE WASHINGTON CARVER. Illustrated. Doubleday, 1951. $1.95. 3–7

A simply written biography, detailed and sympathetic but not adulatory. The author gives a balanced picture of Carver as a scientist and as a person. Indexed.

STEVENSON, AUGUSTA. GEORGE CARVER: BOY SCIENTIST. Bobbs, $2.25. (Text ed. $1.96) (Childhood of Americans series) 3–4

This introduction to the life of Carver is useful for beginning independent readers.

WHITE, ANNE TERRY. GEORGE WASHINGTON CARVER: THE STORY OF A GREAT AMERICAN. Illustrated by Douglas Gorsline. Random, 1953. $1.95. (Library binding $2.28 net) (Landmark books) 6–8

A skillfully written biography of the self-effacing genius whose work changed the economy of the South.

Lydia Maria Child

MELTZER, MILTON. TONGUE OF FLAME: THE LIFE OF LYDIA MARIA CHILD. Crowell, 1965. $3.95. Junior High

A stirring biography of a little-known nineteenth-century fighter for civil rights who founded and edited the first children's magazine, *Juvenile Miscellany*, and was involved in many of the reform movements. This timely biography of an outstanding woman in the struggle of the earlier period will give young people an important perspective and better understanding of today's civil rights movement.

Prudence Crandall

YATES, ELIZABETH. PRUDENCE CRANDALL: WOMAN OF COURAGE. Dutton, 1955. $3.75. 7 and up

This story, about the young Quaker girl who opened her school to Negro girls, will appeal to teenagers. It will be useful as a reminder that the struggle for human rights is by no means new.

Jean Baptiste Pointe de Sable

GRAHAM, SHIRLEY. JEAN BAPTISTE POINTE DE SABLE: FOUNDER OF CHICAGO. Messner, 1953. $3.25. (Library binding $3.19 net) Junior High

Born in the West Indies, educated in France, de Sable came to New Orleans dreaming of the freedom to trade. Eventually he set sail in his own ship, became a friend of Chief Pontiac, and built his home on the shores of Lake Michigan, becoming the first citizen of Chicago.

This absorbing, detailed biography has a wide historical scope.

Frederick Douglass

BONTEMPS, ARNA. FREDERICK DOUGLASS: SLAVE, FIGHTER, FREEMAN. Illustrated. Knopf, 1959. Library binding $3.19 net. 5–9

A vivid, dramatic account of an ex-slave whose philosophy and actions continue to have great meaning in today's society.

DOUGLASS, FREDERICK. LIFE AND TIMES OF FREDERICK DOUGLASS. ed. by Barbara Ritchie. Crowell, 1966. $3.95. Junior High

An excellent adaptation of the last revision (1892) by the author of a book first published in 1842, when he was twenty-five years old. The moving and majestic story of Douglass's escape from slavery and his rise to prominence as a writer, speaker, and postbellum statesman keeps, in this adaptation, the dignity and the lucidity of the original.

GRAHAM, SHIRLEY. THERE WAS ONCE A SLAVE: THE HEROIC STORY OF FREDERICK DOUGLASS. Messner, 1947. $3.95. Junior High

For older readers than the biography by Bontemps.

Paul Laurence Dunbar

GOULD, JEAN. THAT DUNBAR BOY. Illustrated by Charles Walker. Dodd, 1958. $3.25. 5 and up

Paul Laurence Dunbar was born in a little Ohio country town. His mother was a runaway slave with a gift for storytelling. Paul did well in school, wrote poetry constantly, and soon had his work published. In his brief thirty years, he achieved a reputation as a poet, journalist, and novelist.

Well written and inspiring.

Amos Fortune

YATES, ELIZABETH. AMOS FORTUNE: FREE MAN. Illustrated by Nora Unwin. Dutton, 1950. $3.25. Junior High

A beautifully written biography of a little-known Negro. Brought from Africa and sold as a slave, he achieved recognition as a craftsman and citizen in the small town of Joffrey, New Hampshire.

Awarded the Newbery Medal in 1951 for the most distinguished book of literary quality.

Matthew Henson

RIPLEY, SHELDON. MATTHEW HENSON: ARCTIC HERO. Illustrated by E. Harper Johnson. Houghton, 1966. Library binding $2.20 net. 5–7

Matthew Henson was the Negro who accompanied the famous explorer, Commodore Peary, to the North Pole. This is an easy-to-read story of the expedition and Henson's part in it. *To the Top of the World,* by Pauline Angell, also contains a biography of Henson and is reviewed elsewhere in this book.

Martin Luther King, Jr.

CLAYTON, EDWARD T. MARTIN LUTHER KING: THE PEACEFUL WARRIOR. Illustrated by David Hodges. Prentice, 1964. $3.50 4–6

This short biography of a great American leader and Nobel Prize winner (1964) gives the highlights of his childhood, his college days, and his long struggle for equal rights for the Negro. It ends with the passage of the 1964 civil rights law.

The illustrations are interesting, and the straightforward style will make it useful with slow readers. The words and music to "We Shall Overcome" are appended.

Lucretia Mott

STERLING, DOROTHY. LUCRETIA MOTT: GENTLE WARRIOR. Doubleday, 1964. $3.50 Junior High

As her children were growing, Lucretia was a Quaker preacher, and when money was needed she taught school. There were many wrongs in the world, but she soon decided that the greatest wrong was slavery and devoted herself to the cause of emancipation of two million slaves. She aided Benjamin Lundy and William Lloyd Garrison and bought food and clothing from Free Produce stores. In 1833 she joined the Anti-Slavery Society "to deliver our land from its deadliest curse and to secure to the colored population all the rights and privileges which belong to them as Americans."

She was also active in the struggle for women's rights, religious tolerance, and social reforms in America and abroad. After the Civil War, she refused to sit inside a horsecar during a driving rain when a Negro woman was made to stay on the platform. To her eighty-seventh year she worked for the rights of men and women.

Robert Smalls

STERLING, DOROTHY. CAPTAIN OF THE PLANTER: THE STORY OF ROBERT SMALLS. Illustrated by Ernest Crichlow. Doubleday, 1958. $3.50. Junior High

A powerful and dramatic biography of a neglected hero of the Civil War. Smalls, born a slave, piloted a captured Confederate boat past the guns of Fort Sumter and delivered it to the Union forces. Later he became a leader of his people and was sent to Congress. He suffered humiliation during Reconstruction because he refused to compromise his principles.

Important, not only as a biography of a neglected American hero, but for its honest and realistic picture of the period.

Harriet Beecher Stowe

WISE, WINIFRED. HARRIET BEECHER STOWE: WOMAN WITH A CAUSE. Illustrated. Putnam, 1965. $3.50. (Library binding $3.29 net) 6–9

Although she had never been politically militant, Harriet Beecher Stowe felt impelled to plead, in *Uncle Tom's Cabin*, for an end to an institution she detested. She never imagined that her dramatic appeal would bring her permanent fame and riches.

Examines both the subject's personality and her literary career.

Howard Thurman

YATES, ELIZABETH. HOWARD THURMAN: PORTRAIT OF A PRACTICAL DREAMER. Day, 1964. $4.95. Junior High

A biography of an important and revered religious leader, the first Negro to serve as dean of a chapel of a university in the North. This is a detailed account, well organized, with little fictionalization.

Appended are a list of Dr. Thurman's writings, a list of books he used most, and an index.

Tituba

PETRY, ANN. TITUBA OF SALEM VILLAGE. Crowell, 1964. $3.75. Junior High

The slave Tituba, who was brought to Salem from her home in Barbados, has appeared before in literature—in Arthur Miller's *Crucible* and Marion Starkey's *Devil in Massachusetts.* In Ann Petry's fictionalized biography, she is presented with great simplicity and beauty of spirit against a background of hysteria, suspicion, bigotry, and hatred.

The author has achieved a gripping suspense and wonderful character portrait in spite of her controlled, understated style. In spite of her master's cruelty, Tituba retains her competence, serenity, and dignity, even through the cruel witchcraft trial.

Readers of *The Witch of Blackbird Pond* by Elizabeth Speare will find added insight into the Salem witchcraft trials of 1692.

Harriet Tubman

BRADFORD, SARAH. HARRIET TUBMAN: THE MOSES OF HER PEOPLE. Citadel, 1961. Paper $1.25 (Corinth Books) 6–9

Harriet Tubman, an illiterate slave, made nineteen thrilling journeys deep into the South to escort 300 slaves to freedom. She was sent to the South by Governor Andrew of Massachusetts at the beginning of the Civil War to act as a spy for the Union Army; she also served as a hospital nurse. Because of a head injury inflicted by her master that caused sudden fits of sleep, Harriet was considered stupid; yet a sum of $40,000 was offered by slaveholders as a reward for her capture. The book deals mostly with the clever and hair-raising details of her pilgrimages but also stresses her fervent religious motivation.

The style is simple. Much use of Negro dialect adds a lyric tone. Easy enough for the slow, rich enough for the advanced; some may have trouble with the dialect.

McGOVERN, ANN. RUNAWAY SLAVE: THE STORY OF HARRIET TUBMAN. Illustrated by R. M. Powers. Four Winds Press (Scholastic), 1965. $2.50. (Library binding $2.97 net; paper $.45) 3–4

A simply told biography of Harriet Tubman which gives a vivid account of her role as a conductor on the Underground Railroad. Although written for third and fourth graders, it can be used with slow or reluctant older readers.

PETRY, ANN. HARRIET TUBMAN: CONDUCTOR ON THE UNDERGROUND RAILWAY. Crowell, 1955. $3.95. Junior High

Ann Petry has created a portrait of a very real person by emphasizing the character and personality of Harriet Tubman, whose unshakeable faith led her to guide hundreds of slaves to freedom by the Underground Railroad. This carefully documented account includes details not found in other juvenile biographies of Harriet Tubman. The large amount of explicit detail slows up the story, making it more suitable for mature readers.

STERLING, DOROTHY. FREEDOM TRAIN: THE STORY OF HARRIET TUBMAN. Illustrated. Doubleday, 1954. $3.25. 5–8

A first-rate biography of Harriet Tubman, "conductor" on the Underground Railroad, written by the distinguished author of many books on Negro history.

For younger readers than the Tubman biography by Ann Petry.

SWIFT, HILDEGARDE. RAILROAD TO FREEDOM. Harcourt, 1932. $3.95. Junior High

This fictionalized life of Harriet Tubman was a forerunner of its kind. Although it is a well-written story, it remains very difficult to read because of the accurate reproduction of the dialect of the period.

Booker T. Washington

GRAHAM, SHIRLEY. BOOKER T. WASHINGTON: EDUCATOR OF HAND, HEAD AND HEART. Messner, 1955. $3.25. (Library binding $3.19 net) Junior High

A well-written and detailed biography based on Washington's own writings.

STEVENSON, AUGUSTA. BOOKER T. WASHINGTON: AMBITIOUS BOY. Bobbs, 1950. $2.25. (Text ed. $1.96) (Childhood of Americans series) 3–4

Useful as an easy-to-read introduction to the life of the great Negro educator, founder of Tuskegee Institute. Deals mainly with his early years.

WASHINGTON, BOOKER T. UP FROM SLAVERY: AN AUTOBIOGRAPHY OF BOOKER T. WASHINGTON. Doubleday, 1933. $4.50. Paper (Dell) $.45. Junior High

The classic autobiography.

Phillis Wheatley

GRAHAM, SHIRLEY. THE STORY OF PHILLIS WHEATLEY. Illustrated by Robert Burns. Messner, 1949. $3.25. (Library binding $3.19 net) Junior High

In Boston, in 1761, Mrs. Wheatley bought Phillis, a five-year-old slave girl. She taught her to read and write; by fifteen, Phillis was translating Ovid. Because of her original poetry, she was received in the best drawing rooms of Boston and London. She met George Washington and Tom Paine. In the third and blackest year of the War, the elder Wheatleys died and their house was sold to creditors. Phillis's young husband, John Peters, was unable to support her because of the hard times. Her son died, and, not much later, the young Phillis Wheatley Peters died too, alone.

The language is simple; the illustrations have an old-fashioned "etched" appearance. There is just enough history to add flavor without detracting from the main characters.

Poetry, Folklore, and Music

This art of reading is an acquirement which means more than the pronunciation of words, more than repetition of sentences. If it indeed plays an important part in education itself and leads the way to a broad, deep culture, it is no art to be neglected or lightly regarded. Let us encourage and direct it, let us count it worthy of devotion and sacrifice.

—ALICE JORDAN, 1907 (quoted in Frances Clark Sayers, *Summoned by Books*)

Poetry

BONTEMPS, ARNA, editor. GOLDEN SLIPPERS: AN ANTHOLOGY OF NEGRO POETRY. Illustrated. Harper, 1941. $3.95. All grades

An unusually fine selection of the classics of Negro poetry for young readers; a must for every library.

BROOKS, GWENDOLYN. BRONZEVILLE BOYS AND GIRLS. Illustrated by Ronni Solbert. Harper, 1956. $2.50. 2–6

A delightful collection of poems about city children by the well-known Negro poet and Pulitzer Prize winner. The scene is Chicago, but it could be any city or children of any background. This poet has a gift for reproducing the emotions of childhood. The illustrations add to the appeal of the book.

CULLEN, COUNTEE. ON THESE I STAND. Harper, 1947. $3.95. Junior High

What the poet considered to be the best of his poetry.

CULVER, ELOISE. GREAT AMERICAN NEGROES IN VERSE, 1723–1965. Illustrated by Lois Mailou Jones. Associated, 1966. $4.50. K–6

This book contains forty-one short poems on Negro history from Crispus Attucks, one of the first Americans to die in the American Revolution, to James Meredith, the first Negro to graduate from the University of Mississippi. Also included are Ralph Bunche, Mary McLeod Bethune, Katherine Ferguson, George Washington Carver, Phillis Wheatley, Frederick Douglass, Jackie Robinson, Joe Louis, Marian Anderson, and others.

Although the title suggests only Negroes, included are poems about Abraham Lincoln and Henry Wadsworth Longfellow, as well as about Negro spirituals, freedom riders, and the Underground Railroad.

In the foreword the author, a dedicated teacher, makes a plea for the total history of America, so that every child can enjoy "that beauty which is Brotherhood."

DUNBAR, PAUL LAURENCE. COMPLETE POEMS OF PAUL LAURENCE DUNBAR. Illustrated. Dodd, 1940. $4.50. All grades

Contains the complete poems of our country's most celebrated Negro poet of the late nineteenth and early twentieth centuries. A classic of Negro poetry.

———. LITTTLE BROWN BABY. Edited by Bertha Rodgers. Illustrated. Dodd, 1940. $2.75. All grades

An excellent selection of Dunbar's poems especially suited for children and young people.

FIELD, RACHEL. PRAYER FOR A CHILD. Illustrated by Elizabeth Orton Jones. Macmillan, 1964. Library binding $3.24 net. All grades

This won the 1945 Caldecott Award for the "most distinguished picture book." Elizabeth Orton Jones illustrates Rachel Field's poem with an appealing picture of all types of children—indeed a realistic interpretation of "God bless children everywhere."

HUGHES, LANGSTON. THE DREAM KEEPER AND OTHER POEMS. Illustrated. Knopf, 1932. Library binding $2.79 net. 8 and up

Hughes has made a selection of his poems especially suitable for teenagers. Some have been recorded by him for Folkways Records (FP104).

———, and ARNA BONTEMPS. THE POETRY OF THE NEGRO, 1746–1949. Doubleday, 1949. $6.50. Junior High

Includes selected poems from over sixty American Negro poets, besides others by non-Negroes and native poets of the Caribbean, Latin America, and Africa, with brief biographies of each poet.

An excellent source book for student and teacher.

MCBROWN, GERTRUDE PARTHENIA. PICTURE POETRY BOOK. Illustrated by Lois Jones. Associated, 1935. $1.40. K–3

Simple verses, attractively illustrated by a Negro artist. One of the earliest works of its kind which is still useful.

NEWSOME, EFFIE LEE. GLADIOLA GARDEN. Illustrated by Lois Jones. Associated, 1940. $2.65. K–3

Poems for younger children by a Negro poet and artist.

ROLLINS, CHARLEMAE HILL, editor. CHRISTMAS GIF'. Illustrated. Follett, 1963. $4.95. All grades

An anthology of Christmas poems, songs, and stories by or about Negroes. Many of the selections are humorous; some are autobiographical; included is a section of Christmas recipes "from the 'Big House' and the cabin." Separate author and title indexes are appended.

SWIFT, HILDEGARDE. NORTH STAR SHINING. Illustrated by Lynd Ward. Morrow, 1947. $3.95. 5 and up

One of the finest books written on Negro history. In moving verse, this author recounts the highlights of the Negro's accomplishments in the history of America. Each character tells his part in building America:

> I built your world, Oh white man,
> But in the building it became mine too!

The many characters make this useful for verse choir, individual dramatic readers, or assembly programs. Full-page colored lithographs enhance the book.

TAYLOR, MARGARET. DID YOU FEED MY COW? Crowell, 1956. (out of print) All grades

Traditional games, rhymes, and riddles of city streets and country lanes compiled by a Chicago teacher.

Folklore

FELTON, HAROLD W. JOHN HENRY AND HIS HAMMER. Illustrated by Aldren A. Watson. Knopf, 1950. $4.00. (Library binding $3.29 net) 5–9

John Henry is a Negro legendary hero who helped to build the first railroads linking the East and West. This is excellent for younger children and useful for slow readers in the upper grades. It may be used as supplementary social studies material on pioneers or simply as ballad or folklore material.

GIPSON, FRED. TRAIL–DRIVING ROOSTER. Illustrated by Marc Simont. Harper, 1955. $2.95. All grades

Boisterous tall tale about a rooster whose fighting spirit saves him from the frying pan. This excellent read-aloud story has all the flavor of the authentic American tall tale.

KEATS, EZRA JACK. JOHN HENRY: AN AMERICAN LEGEND. Illustrated by the author. Pantheon, 1965. $3.50. (Library binding $3.39 net) K–3

A simplified picturebook version of the legend of the Negro folk hero which lends itself to reading aloud. Superb illustrations.

WHITING, HELEN ADELE. NEGRO FOLK TALES FOR PUPILS IN THE PRIMARY GRADES. Illustrated. Associated, 1939. $1.40. K–3

This is a very simple retelling of many familiar animal stories of African origin. The large type and attractive black and white drawings make the book particularly appealing to the early grades. The author is a distinguished Negro teacher and writer of Negro history.

Music

BLACK AND WHITE. Words and drawings by David Arkin; music by Earl Robinson. Ritchie, 1966. $2.95. (Library binding $2.92 net) 2–7

A dramatic song, a story about freedom to go to school together, is the focus of this book. Edward R. Murrow used it in 1960 on a program to focus attention on the problems of desegregation. The simple words are illustrated with alternating stark black and white pages until the last two pages, where color is introduced to add an optimistic note. The music is included at the back of the book.

HUGHES, LANGSTON. FIRST BOOK OF JAZZ. Pictures by Cliff Roberts; Music selected by David Martin. Watts, 1954. $2.65. 4 and up

From African drums, work songs, blues, jazz, boogie-woogie, and Louis Armstrong, Langston Hughes tells the story of jazz. "Jazz is a way of playing," he says, and in his text he explains this way with musical scores, lyrics, and illustrations. The many clever woodcuts are as enjoyable and instructive as the text.

A good book for the young *aficionado.*

JOHNSON, JAMES WELDON, and J. ROSAMOND JOHNSON. THE BOOKS OF AMERICAN NEGRO SPIRITUALS (2 vols.). Viking, 1940. $6.95.

One hundred and twenty-four favorite spirituals arranged for voice and piano. Excellent also for family participation as well as classroom use.

MYRUS, DONALD. BALLADS, BLUES, AND THE BIG BEAT. Illustrated with photographs. Macmillan, 1966. $3.95. (Library binding $3.94 net) Junior High

A survey of folk songs in this country, with an occasional nod to performers of other kinds of music. Plentifully illustrated with photographs, this is a knowledgeable, chatty, and subjective discussion of the genre, the composers, the performers, and the audience. Many of the great folk song artists described are Negro. A list of records and an index are included.

TRENT-JOHNS, ALTONA. PLAY SONGS OF THE DEEP SOUTH. Associated, 1944. $2.65. All grades

The author's foreword notes that these twelve "play songs" have been sung and danced by Negro children throughout the South; they have been arranged simply so that young pianists as well as teachers of folk dancing can use them.

WHITING, HELEN ADELE. NEGRO ART, MUSIC AND RHYME. Illustrated. Associated, 1938. $1.40. K–3

This social science reader describes works of the African Negroes.

Science*

Every child has the right to see himself and life as he knows it reflected in a book. Only in this way can he feel that his culture and people have worth and a place in the eyes of others. Similarly, every child has the right to venture, through books, out of his own sphere into a wider world where he can encounter people different from himself. The wider the variety of children a young reader can meet in books, the more exciting the world can become for him.

—JEAN KARL (quoted in *Interracial Books for Children*)

GOLDIN, AUGUSTA. STRAIGHT HAIR, CURLY HAIR. Illustrated by Ed Emberley. Crowell, 1966. $3.25. (Library binding $2.96 net) (Let's-Read-and-Find-Out book) K–3

An easy-to-read scientific explanation of why some hair is straight and some curly. The humorous drawings add interest to a subject about which most children are curious.

LERNER, MARGUERITE RUSH. RED MAN, WHITE MAN, AFRICAN CHIEF: THE STORY OF SKIN COLOR. Illustrated. Lerner, 1960. $2.75. 1–5

A good introduction to the reason for difference in skin color. The style is objective and simple, and the book is well illustrated.

SELSAM, MILLICENT E. TONY'S BIRDS. Illustrated by Kurt Werth. Harper, 1961. $1.95. (Library binding $2.19 net; paper $.88) (I Can Read book) K–3

Tony becomes interested in bird-watching on a walk with his father. The author successfully combines story life and scientifically accurate information. The illustrations show that Tony is a Negro.

SHOWERS, PAUL. LOOK AT YOUR EYES. Illustrated by Paul Galdone. Crowell, 1962. $3.25. (Library binding $2.96 net) (Let's-Read-and-Find-Out book) K–3

Children learn through easy text and attractive illustrations some of the basic facts about eyes. The child pictured is a Negro, and comparison of eye color is made by picturing his friends.

---

*See also biographies of scientists under Individual Biographies.

————. YOUR SKIN AND MINE. Illustrated by Paul Galdone. Crowell, 1965. $3.25. (Library binding $2.96 net) (Let's-Read-and-Find-Out book) K–3

The simple, brief text and attractive illustrations present the facts about skin and its function, including color differences, the dermis and epidermis, hair follicles, pores, sensation and temperature adjustments, etc. Uses boys of different color as examples. Large print and attractive format.

STERNE, EMMA GELDERS. BLOOD BROTHERS: FOUR MEN OF SCIENCE. Illustrated by Oscar Liebman. Knopf, 1959. $3.00. 5–8

Dramatic biographies of four scientists whose discoveries enlarged our knowledge of blood. Includes Charles Drew, the Negro scientist, who was first to find the method for processing raw blood into plasma for instant transfusions.

Sports

Real reading experiences are done with our brains and our hearts, not only with our eyes. And such experiences can come only from books which have integrity, style, and a portion of the fundamental truth of life. They are found in books written by men and women who respect youth, who have an innate appreciation of the ability of young people to recognize quality when it is offered them.

—DOROTHY BRODERICK, *The Bookmark*

General Nonfiction

BELL, JOSEPH N. OLYMPIC THRILLS. Messner, 1965. $3.95. (Library binding $3.64 net) 6 and up

Olympic winners from the United States have included Negroes in many of the events each year. Included here are Jesse Owens, broad jumping and running; Harrison Dillard, sprint; Bob Mathaias, decathlon; Bob Richards, pole vault; John McMarten, U.S. hockey team; Billy Mills, long distance long shot; and Wilma Rudolph and Althea Gibson. The writing style is absorbing.

ROBINSON, RAY. GREATEST WORLD SERIES THRILLERS. Illustrated. Random, 1965. $1.95. (Library binding $2.28 net) 4–7

Not unusual material, but dramatic stories of a dozen particularly exciting baseball games. One account of the 1954 game between the Dodgers and the Indians tells of the game in which Willie Mays made one of the greatest catches of baseball history.

Collective Biography

BONTEMPS, ARNA. FAMOUS NEGRO ATHLETES. Illustrated with photographs. Dodd, 1964. $3.50. Junior High

Biographical sketches of Joe Louis, Sugar Ray Robinson, Jackie Robinson, Satchel Paige, Willie Mays, Jesse Owens, Wilt Chamberlain, Jim Brown, and Althea Gibson. Although the emphasis is on sports achievements, the author does give a good account of their personal lives. It was such athletes as these who helped change the image of the Negro. A popular collection.

GELMAN, STEVE. YOUNG OLYMPIC CHAMPIONS. Illustrated with photographs. Norton, 1964. $3.50. (Library binding $3.58 net) 6–9

A collection of eleven biographies which includes boxing champion

Cassius Clay and Wilma Rudolph, track star. Other Negro stars are mentioned in connection with particular sports and may be traced through the index.

Individual Sports Biographies and Autobiographies

Arthur Ashe

ROBINSON, LOUIE, JR. ARTHUR ASHE: TENNIS CHAMPION. Doubleday, 1967. $2.95. 6 and up

Arthur Ashe, a lonely little boy after the death of his mother, spent most of his time in the segregated city park of Richmond, Virginia, where his father worked. There, a sympathetic playground director saw his possibilities as a tennis player and introduced the boy and his father to Dr. Walter Johnson, a Negro physician and tennis enthusiast, who provided a court and instruction.

Ashe became the first Negro man to play on the U.S. Davis Cup Team, where he performed brilliantly in England and Australia. On his return he was invited to appear before the state legislature in his home town, where he had once been refused admittance to a movie theatre. Highly recommended.

Jim Brown

TERZIAN, JAMES P. THE JIMMY BROWN STORY. Messner, 1964. $3.25. (Library binding $3.19 net) Junior High

Biography of a star football player in college and later with the Cleveland Browns professional team.

KLEIN, LARRY. JIM BROWN, THE RUNNING BACK. Putnam, 1965. $3.50. (Library binding $3.29 net) Junior High

Heavily saturated with detailed descriptions of football games. The writing is mildly effusive and occasionally humorous; Brown's spectacular career does not need the dramatic treatment given here, but it will probably interest sports fans nevertheless. Several photographs are included; Brown's impressive list of records and an index are appended.

Roy Campanella

CAMPANELLA, ROY. IT'S GOOD TO BE ALIVE. Illustrated. Little, 1959. $5.00. Junior High

During his convalescence from the tragic accident that ended his baseball days, Roy Campanella recalls the highlights of his career. His courageous struggle to overcome the enormous physical handicap is vividly described, and the sharing of this courage with others shows his concern for his fellow men and gratitude to be alive.

The autobiography presents a complete picture of his life instead of limiting itself to baseball activities.

Cassius Clay

SULLIVAN, GEORGE. THE CASSIUS CLAY STORY. Illustrated. Fleet, 1964. $3.95. Junior High

The story of the colorful career of the famous heavyweight fighter who started boxing at the age of twelve to learn to thrash a boy who had stolen his bicycle. For older readers.

Althea Gibson

GIBSON, ALTHEA. I ALWAYS WANTED TO BE SOMEBODY. Photographs. Harper, 1958. $3.95. (Library binding $3.79 net; paper $.60) Junior High

From the first sentence to the end, this lively, intimate account is more than a sports story; it is the story of a personality. Althea Gibson tells of her life in Harlem, a life of enduring poverty. She includes her "discovery" and presents a complete account of her high school years in North Carolina, college years at Florida A & M College, her break into professional tennis, and her first match at Forest Hills, as well as her enlistment in the WACS, her European and Asian tour for the State Department, and winning the world's tennis championship.

Will hold the interest of advanced readers.

Willie Mays

EINSTEIN, CHARLES. WILLIE MAYS: COAST TO COAST GIANT. Illustrated. Putnam, 1963. Junior High

A rambling account of Mays's career with very little biographical information but heavy emphasis on games, individual plays, peripheral anecdotes, etc. Adulatory, breezy, and disorganized, but with some colorful writing and with, of course, an appealing subject. Mays's records through 1962 are appended, as is an index.

HANO, ARNOLD. WILLIE MAYS. Grosset, 1966. $1.95. (Library binding $2.49 net; paper $.50) Junior High

Only the fact that Willie Mays *is* an exciting baseball player makes this book palatable. The text is gushy, disorganized, and repetitive—and, here and there, amusing. The author informs the reader that Mays is exciting with the regularity and enthusiasm of a television commercial, but his descriptions of games or great plays may be enjoyed by fans. An appended page cites Mays's lifetime batting record.

SCHOOR, GENE. WILLIE MAYS, MODEST CHAMPION. Putnam, 1960. $3.50. 5–9

A fast-moving biography of a baseball hero.

SHAPIRO, MILTON J. THE WILLIE MAYS STORY. Illustrated. Messner, 1960. $3.25. (Library binding $3.19 net) Junior High

For more mature readers than the Schoor biography.

Leroy (Satchel) Paige

PAIGE, SATCHEL, and DAVID LIPMAN. MAYBE I'LL PITCH FOREVER. Illustrated. Doubleday, 1962. $4.50. Junior High

Satchel Paige came from the slums of Mobile, Alabama, to travel the baseball circuits of the United States and Mexico until he became a major league pitcher. A happy second marriage and his pitching ability enabled Paige to overcome his early selfishness and irresponsibility.

Provides a picture of the Negro baseball leagues and the problems of the Negro player in joining the major leagues.

Floyd Patterson

PATTERSON, FLOYD, and MILTON GROSS. VICTORY OVER MYSELF. Random, 1962. $3.95. Paper (Scholastic) $.50. 7 and up

This is the account of a young New York delinquent who, after spending two years in a correctional house, later succeeded in capturing the heavyweight boxing championship. Patterson was the youngest Negro ever to attain the crown and the first to regain it.

This is the story not only of the man who won the world championship but also of the man who overcame the handicap of an underprivileged and painful childhood. Patterson's statements of his beliefs can be used to suggest compositions. There are many references to schools, streets, and other places familiar to New Yorkers.

Jackie Robinson

ROBINSON, JACKIE, and ALFRED DUCKETT. BREAKTHROUGH TO THE BIG LEAGUE. Illustrated. Harper, 1965. $3.50. (Library binding $3.27 net) 5–9

A surprisingly good book, told with frankness, humor, and warmth. Born with a naturally quick temper and an innate sense of dignity, Robinson was quick to react to insults—and there were many during his pre-baseball days. When he became the first Negro in the major leagues, the abuse increased to torrents. He held his temper as he was asked to do, and he admits that it was his respect for Branch Rickey and Rickey's faith in and support of him that sustained him.

Not the typical baseball biography, this is a story of courage.

ROBINSON, JACKIE, and CARL T. ROWAN. WAIT TILL NEXT YEAR. Illustrated. Random, 1960. $4.95. Junior High

A biography of the well-known baseball player written by a distinguished Negro.

SHAPIRO, MILTON J. JACKIE ROBINSON OF THE BROOKLYN DODGERS. Illustrated with photographs. Messner, 1957. $3.25. (Library binding $3.19 net) 6–10

The story of Jackie Robinson's introduction to professional baseball, his tumultuous years of striving, and his triumph. The reader gets a picture of a determined, hard-working man with a sense of justice. Robinson's home life as a child is covered, but little of his personal life as an adult is included. The last part of the book concentrates on baseball.

The story of Robinson's career could hardly be told without emphasizing his breaking the color line; however, this theme is not so treated.

Maury Wills

WILLS, MAURY, and STEVE GARDNER. IT PAYS TO STEAL. Illustrated. Prentice, 1963. $3.95. Junior High

The ingredients of success are courage, ability, industry, and determination. This detailed account of Wills's baseball career portrays his generous share of each, including a strong religious belief. He is anxious to share his know-how with beginners.

Sports Fiction

BISHOP, CURTIS KENT. LITTLE LEAGUE HEROES. Lippincott, 1960. Library binding $3.39 net. 3–7

With hard work and his father's help, Joel Carroll makes a Little League team. This is Texas, and Joel is a Negro. The influential grandfather of a team member withdraws his grandson and his financial support. Joel is beaten up and the clubhouse is ransacked.

The situations are rather pat and Joel is incredibly patient, but attitudes are good and the detailed baseball sequences are well written.

DECKER, DUANE WALTER. HIT AND RUN. Morrow, 1949. $3.50. Junior High

More than a good sports story, this is about two players new to the big league, who have serious problems to face. One of them, Chip Fiske, is an undersized fielder with a vicious temper; the other is the first Negro to break into the league. The games and the behind-the-scenes life of the players are exciting and fast-moving, and the sympathetic treatment of the two men's personality problems and how they help each other adds another dimension.

Some of the incidents are similar to those faced by Jackie Robinson during his first year with the Dodgers.

FRICK, CONSTANCE H. TOURNEY TEAM. Harcourt, 1954. $3.25. Junior High

Rocky Ryan is removed from the high school basketball team because of poor sportsmanship and a quick temper. He finally becomes the sports reporter for the school paper. Reporting the tournament games, he learns compassion and respect for his fellow man. The coach gives him another chance on the team which promises Rocky another try at basketball during his senior year. Easy reading.

The reader is made too aware that the Negro players are Negroes rather than basketball players.

HAYES, FLORENCE S. SKID. Illustrated by Elton C. Fax. Houghton, 1948. $3.25. 5–7

Still popular, in spite of some inaccuracies in the baseball plays.

HEUMAN, WILLIAM. BACKCOURT MAN. Dodd, 1960. $2.95. Junior High

Richie Harrigan, basketball star from Henderson Teachers College, is unusually short for a professional player, but he signs a contract with the Panthers. Richie, a Negro, and Ben, an Italian, are a fast, powerful, winning basketball combination and good friends. Their efforts uncover a plot to ruin the Panthers' league standing, forcing the club to be sold at a low price. Fast, professional basketball is the entire story.

JACKSON, JESSE. ANCHOR MAN. Illustrated. Harper, 1947. Library binding $2.92 net. (sequel to *Call Me Charley*) 5–9

By his senior year, Charley is secure with his friends and school, but the new students from the "Blackberry Patch" bring prejudices, jealousies, and misunderstandings. Charley's attitude toward fair play and justice remains firm, and he rises above the problems to win the track meet, bringing honor to his school and race.

Most valuable is the portrayal of the varying attitudes of the Negro toward his problems.

————. CALL ME CHARLEY. Illustrated. Harper, 1945. $2.95. (Library binding $2.92 net) 5–9

When twelve-year-old Charley moves into a white neighborhood, he faces rejection and discrimination. His mother is ambitious for him, but the indifference of his uneducated father intensifies his school problems. Tom, his white friend, believes in Charley, and this supplies the strength necessary to help Charley succeed at school and find some happiness in his spare time.

LEONARD, BURGESS. REBOUND MAN. Watts, 1962. $2.95. Junior High

Ross Lundsford wants to play high school basketball but must work part-time; he is able to join the team when he gets a new job with different hours. He loses his old job, driving the school bus, because the bus is burned as a warning to the school authorities against school integration. The Negro, Wade, is a quiet and courageous boy who feels that he must, as a representative of his race, show no hostility. Ross, Wade's best friend, fights for his acceptance; so do the local editor and his daughter and a few others, but most of the citizens are hostile. Wade is accepted after he rescues some small children who are trapped in another bus accident.

The ending is rather pat, and the book has a few too many themes, but this is an unusual sports story, especially in its emphasis on educational goals (even from the coach).

QUIGLEY, MARTIN. TODAY'S GAME. Viking, 1965. $3.95.
Junior High

A better-than-average sports story told from a manager's point of view. The action is mainly concerned with one game; Barney Mann comes close to losing his job as manager of the Blue Jays when he trades his old friend, a veteran Hall of Fame pitcher, for a young Negro outfielder. The new player seems to be in a slump, and Barney must help him or see his team lose. The unsentimental and straightforward handling of the problem makes this good reading.

TUNIS, JOHN R. ALL-AMERICAN. Harcourt, 1942. $3.50.
Junior High

Although this school football story is over twenty-five years old, it is still read and enjoyed because some of the problems presented by the first Negro player on a school team are still with us, even though to a lesser degree. The values stressed are the lasting ones, and the writing is clear and vivid.

———. YEA! WILDCATS! Harcourt, 1944. $3.50.
Junior High

A good sports story that serves as a vehicle for an indictment of the corruption in amateur sports. A young basketball coach leads his team to the Indiana state finals and discovers that the tickets are peddled, that there are paid ringers and large-scale betting. He also finds a considerable amount of resentment because one member of the team is Negro. The Negro boy is hospitalized and can't play in the tournament, but the defeat of the team touches off mob hysteria in the home town, and the coach has to break up a racial incident.

Sources

1. THE ASSOCIATED PUBLISHERS, INC., provides, in addition to books, other materials on the study of Negro history for elementary, high school, and adult use. These materials include study kits and sets of pictures of distinguished Negroes, and a study guide arranged by *Four Steps in Negro History:*
   Shackelford, Jane Dabney. *Child's Story of the Negro.* (for teachers and students in elementary school)
   Woodson, Carter G. *Negro Makers of History,* revised by Charles H. Wesley. (for grades 6 and 7)
   Woodson, Carter G., and Charles H. Wesley. *Story of the Negro Retold.* (for high school)
   ————. *Negro in Our History.* (for adults)

Address: 1538 9th Street, N.W.
Washington, D.C. 20001

2. COUNCIL ON INTERRACIAL BOOKS FOR CHILDREN, INC., publishes a quarterly newsletter and "encourages the writing production and effective distribution of books to fill the needs of nonwhite and urban poor children." The Council hopes to establish annual cash awards for the best books in this field.
   Address: 9 East 40th Street
   New York, New York 10016

3. THE NEGRO BIBLIOGRAPHIC AND RESEARCH CENTER, INC., a nonprofit organization, provides a variety of services in Negro research and publishes an annotated bibliography of *The Negro in Print,* including books and pamphlets, fiction and nonfiction, foreign and domestic, bound and unbound, current and past. The bibliography is published every two months by a distinguished staff of research editors and authors of juvenile and adult books on Negro history.
   Address: 117 R Street, N.E.
   Washington, D.C. 20002

Directory of Publishers

Abbreviation	*Address*
Abelard	Abelard-Schuman Limited 6 West 57th Street New York, New York 10019
Afro-American	Afro-American Publishing Co., Inc. 765 East Oakwood Boulevard Chicago, Illinois 60653
Associated	Associated Publishers, Inc. 1538 9th Street, N.W. Washington, D.C. 20001
Atheneum	Atheneum Publishers 162 East 38th Street New York, New York 10016
Berkley	Berkley Publishing Corporation 15 East 26th Street New York, New York 10010
Bobbs	The Bobbs-Merrill Co., Inc. 4300 West 62nd Street Indianapolis, Indiana 46206
Cadmus	Cadmus Library Editions E. M. Hale & Company 1201 South Hastings Way Eau Claire, Wisconsin 54702
Citadel	Citadel Press, Inc. 222 Park Avenue South New York, New York 10003
Coward	Coward-McCann, Inc. 200 Madison Avenue New York, New York 10016
Criterion	Criterion Books, Inc. 6 West 57th Street New York, New York 10019
Crowell	Thomas Y. Crowell Company 201 Park Avenue South New York, New York 10003
Crown	Crown Publishers, Inc. 419 Park Avenue South New York, New York 10016
Day	The John Day Company, Inc. 62 West 45th Street New York, New York 10036
Dial	The Dial Press, Inc. 750 Third Avenue New York, New York 10017

Dodd	Dodd, Mead & Co. 79 Madison Avenue New York, New York 10016
Doubleday	Doubleday & Company, Inc. Garden City New York 11530
Dutton	E. P. Dutton & Co., Inc. 201 Park Avenue South New York, New York 10003
Farrar	Farrar, Straus & Giroux, Inc. 19 Union Square West New York, New York 10003
Fleet	Fleet Publishing Corp. 230 Park Avenue New York, New York 10017
Follett	Follett Publishing Company 1010 West Washington Boulevard Chicago, Illinois 60607
Friendship	Friendship Press 475 Riverside Drive New York, New York 10027
Ginn	Ginn and Company Statler Building, Back Bay P.O. 191 Boston, Massachusetts 02117
Greenberg	Chilton Books 401 Walnut Street Philadelphia, Pennsylvania 19106
Grosset	Grosset & Dunlap, Inc. 51 Madison Avenue New York, New York 10010
Harcourt	Harcourt, Brace & World, Inc. 757 Third Avenue New York, New York 10017
Harper	Harper & Row, Publishers 49 East 33rd Street New York, New York 10016
Hastings	Hastings House, Publishers, Inc. 151 East 50th Street New York, New York 10022
Hill	Hill & Wang, Inc. 141 Fifth Avenue New York, New York 10010
Houghton	Houghton Mifflin Company 2 Park Street Boston, Massachusetts 02107

Knopf	Alfred A. Knopf, Inc. 501 Madison Avenue New York, New York 10022
Knox	John Knox Press 8 N. Sixth Street Box 1176 Richmond, Virginia 23209
Lerner	Lerner Publications Co. 241 First Avenue North Minneapolis, Minnesota 55401
Lippincott	J. B. Lippincott Co. East Washington Square Philadelphia, Pennsylvania 19105
Little	Little, Brown and Company 34 Beacon Street Boston, Massachusetts 02106
Lothrop	Lothrop, Lee & Shepard Co., Inc. 419 Park Avenue South New York, New York 10016
McKay	David McKay Co., Inc. 750 Third Avenue New York, New York 10017
Macmillan	The Macmillan Company 866 Third Avenue New York, New York 10022
Macrae	Macrae Smith Co. 225 South 15th Street Philadelphia, Pennsylvania 19102
Messner	Julian Messner 1 West 39th Street New York, New York 10018
Morrow	William Morrow & Co., Inc. 425 Park Avenue South New York, New York 10016
Norton	W. W. Norton & Company, Inc. 55 Fifth Avenue New York, New York 10003
Pantheon	Pantheon Books, Inc. 22 East 51st Street New York, New York 10022
Parents	Parents' Magazine Press 52 Vanderbilt Avenue New York, New York 10017
Popular	Popular Library, Inc. 355 Lexington Avenue New York, New York 10017

Prentice	Prentice-Hall, Inc. Englewood Cliffs New Jersey 07632
Putnam	G. P. Putnam's Sons 200 Madison Avenue New York, New York 10016
Rand	Rand McNally & Co. Box 7600 Chicago, Illinois 60680
Random	Random House, Inc. 457 Madison Avenue New York, New York 10022
Ritchie	The Ward Ritchie Press 1932 Hyperion Avenue Los Angeles, California 90027
Scholastic	Scholastic Book Services 50 West 44th Street New York, New York 10036
Univ. N.C.	University of North Carolina Press Chapel Hill North Carolina 27515
Vanguard	Vanguard Press, Inc. 424 Madison Avenue New York, New York 10017
Viking	The Viking Press, Inc. 625 Madison Avenue New York, New York 10022
Washburn	Ives Washburn, Inc. 750 Third Avenue New York, New York 10017
Watts	Franklin Watts, Inc. 575 Lexington Avenue New York, New York 10022
Whitman	Albert Whitman & Co. 560 West Lake Street Chicago, Illinois 60606
World	The World Publishing Company 2231 West 110th Street Cleveland, Ohio 44102

Biographies

Authors, Editors, Illustrators

Books